JEWELS OF THE
TSARS

THE ROMANOVS & IMPERIAL RUSSIA

First published in the United States of America in 2006 by

The Vendome Press

1334 York Avenue

New York, N.Y. 10021

Translated from the French by Barbara Mellor

Publishers: Beatrice Vincenzini, Francesco Venturi
Project Managers: David Shannon, U.K.; Sarah Davis, U.S.
Editorial Director: Victor Loupan
Art Director: François Sargologo
Editor: Séverine Courtaud

ISBN-10: 0-86565-171-X
ISBN-13: 978-0-86565-171-5

          Library of Congress Cataloging-in-Publication Data
Michel, Prince of Greece, 1939-
  Jewels of the tsars : the Romanovs and Imperial Russia / Prince Michael of Greece.
      p. cm.
  Includes index.
  ISBN-13: 978-0-86565-171-5 (hardcover : alk. paper)
  ISBN-10: 0-86565-171-X (hardcover : alk. paper)
  1. Romanov, House of–Art collections. 2. Jewelry–Private collections–Russia. I. Title.
  NK7303.R58M53 2006
  739.270947–dc22

                    2006018420

First edition
Printed in France

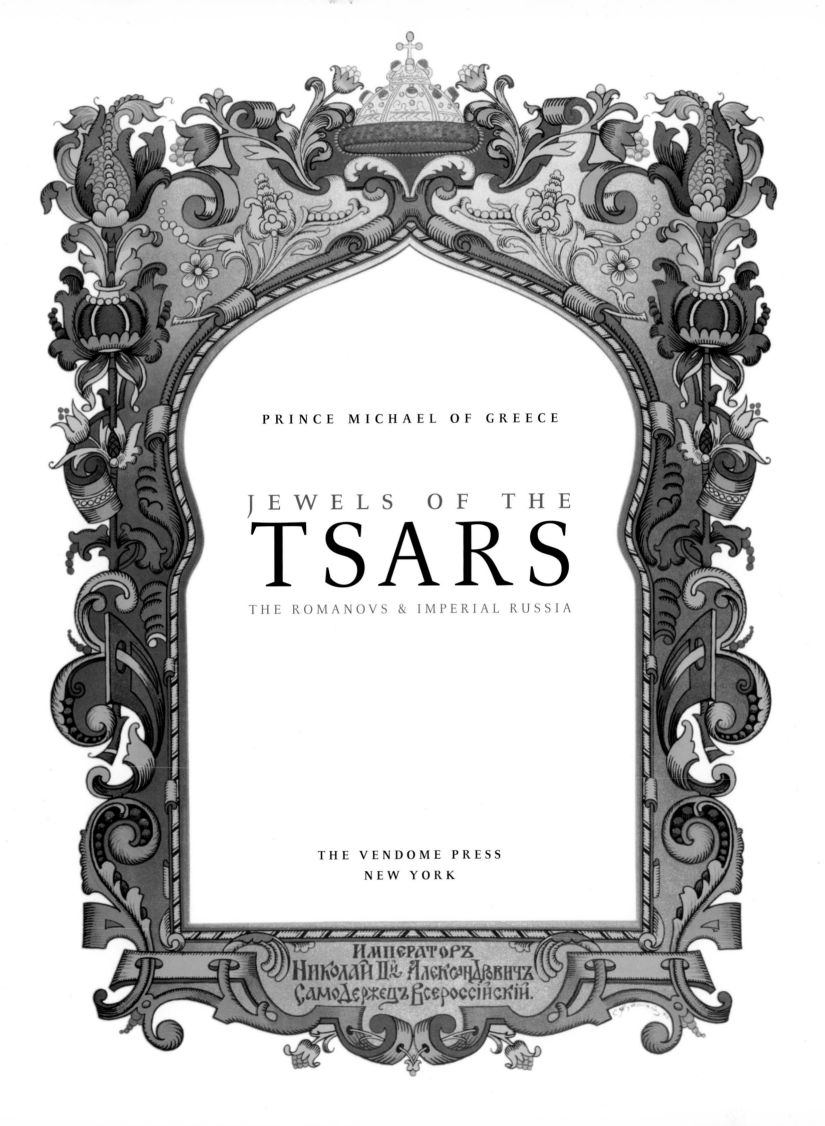

PRINCE MICHAEL OF GREECE

JEWELS OF THE
TSARS

THE ROMANOVS & IMPERIAL RUSSIA

THE VENDOME PRESS
NEW YORK

ИМПЕРАТОРЪ
НИКОЛАЙ IIй АЛЕКСАНДРВИЧЪ
САМОДЕРЖЕЦЪ ВСЕРОССІЙСКІЙ.

For Alexandra & James,
Degenhart, Cosmas
& Dagmar Brown

CONTENTS

Page 4

A PORTRAIT OF EMPRESS ELIZABETH FEODOROVNA OF RUSSIA,
wife of Alexander I, by Jean-Laurent Monnier, 1802.
State Tretyakov Gallery, Moscow

THE CROWN OF MONOMAKH (opposite). Fashioned from gold, pearls and
precious stones and trimmed with sable, this crown, also known as the 'Cap of
Monomakh', remains a powerful symbol of the Russian monarchy. The original
crown formed a link between the Russian tsars and the fabulous emperors of
Byzantium, from whom Vladimir Monomakh, who commissioned this crown in
the late thirteenth or fourteenth century, was descended in the female line. Known
as the 'Crown of Monomakh of the Second Order', the crown shown here is a copy of
the original made in 1682 for the dual coronation of Ivan V and his younger brother
Peter, the future Peter the Great. It is also known as the 'Crown of Kiev Vladimir
Novgorod'.

I can never resist a gripping story: I collect them, and I love to recount them at parties and in my books. The best of them – the ones that are the most extraordinary or unexpected, mysterious or thrilling – are invariably true, taken from the great events of history. And from this inexhaustible seam, I find I am inexorably drawn to stories featuring my own forebears, members of the dynasties who shaped Europe.

I also adore jewellery: not the gaudy creations of modern-day jewellers, but pieces of beauty and history, works of superb craftsmanship and aesthetic inspiration, with their own long and distinguished stories to tell. In these I take an atavistic delight.

These twin passions find their supreme expression in the history of the Russian empire. As a descendant of the Romanovs through my grandmother, Grand Duchess Olga, I take a certain pride in claiming that no other dynasty has ever, in so brief a period – a mere three centuries – lived such an extraordinary litany of tales of love and glory, drama and sensation, adventure and mystery. Nor has any other dynasty ever amassed a collection of jewellery as immense or as breathtaking as the jewels of the Romanovs.

In presenting the Russian imperial jewels within these pages, I hope to share my twin passions with a wider public. In the years since the Revolution of 1917, many of these jewels have been dismantled or dispersed. But through all these vicissitudes, the magic of these fabulous jewels has never failed to enthrall me, as I hope it will my readers.

GRAND DUCHESS ELIZABETH FEODOROVNA.
Unlike most European royal dynasties, the Russian imperial family could boast a bevy of beauties. Lovely though they were, however, few could rival the sheer glamour of Grand Duchess Sergei (known as 'Ella' within the family), who was married to one of Nicholas II's uncles. Here she is shown wearing the costume of a sixteenth-century Russian princess, designed for the famous costume ball held in the Winter Palace in 1903.

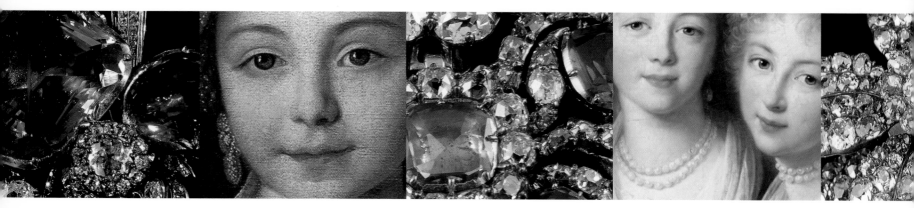

Immeasurably vast and impenetrable, the Russian Empire, which in effect lingered on in the guise of the Soviet Union until the fall of the Iron Curtain, was menacing in its mystery and terrifying in its sheer power. Until they gave way to a string of stolidly unaristocratic presidents, autocratic grand dukes, tsars and emperors held turbulent sway over this fabled, awe-inspiring empire. Yet it had all started from modest beginnings.

The first tribal chief to lay claim to the title of ruler of this land that was to be known as Russia was not even a Russian: Riurik, to whom the majority of the great princely Russian families could trace their ancestry, was a Viking from the tribe of Rus, which gave the land its name. In the centuries that followed, Riurik's successors as ruler of Rus, subjugated by wave upon wave of Mongol invasion from the Asian steppes, were forced to pay homage to the Great Khan of the Golden Horde.

In the fifteenth century, a Russian tsar married a Byzantine princess, thereby throwing off the Tatar yoke and ensuring a new prominence for Moscow. The Tsarigrad of the Slavs now rose to become the 'Third Rome', after Constantinople. But despite this august affiliation, a number of the Russian tsars who followed remained firmly under the sway of eastern influence, and almost all of them remained unrepentantly barbaric in their ways.

A vicious and ceaseless round of coups d'état, assassinations and massacres plunged the empire into an abyss of savagery and violence, as encapsulated in the despotic reigns of Ivan the Terrible and Boris Godunov, who were every bit as monstrous in fact as they are heroic in film and opera. The blood-spattered setting against which these scenes of murder and butchery were played out so relentlessly was one of gilded splendour, however, for the tsars – few of whom were destined for a natural death – were fastidious in their creation of courts of extreme and ostentatious extravagance. Like the Byzantine emperors before them, they realized that their prestige depended upon the quality and sheer volume of their jewelry. Accordingly, they decked themselves in jewels from head to toe.

As the tsarinas lived largely in seclusion, in the eastern manner, it fell to the men to display this wealth, making their ceremonial appearances in shimmering full-length kaftans of silk brocade, laden with crowns, chains, bracelets and sceptres. Though of primitive workmanship, these treasures were set with cabochons of monstrous size, powerful and impressive. Like the great Indian moguls and Ottoman sultans, the tsars inhabited a world encrusted with jewels, even down to their weapons and the harnesses of their horses.

It was in the sixteenth century, when Russia was still stuck in the Middle Ages, that the first Romanovs made their appearance. Their story too grew from modest beginnings. The first tsar of the new dynasty, Mikhail, son of the future Russian patriarch Filaret, was put on the throne in 1613 precisely because he was bland in character and generally inoffensive. Contrary to all expectations, however, he and his successors succeeded in imposing order, in pacifying the troublesome and rebellious boyars, and

in unifying the land over which they ruled. As a result they were able to extend their dominions in all directions, in an expansionist movement that, once started, gained its own momentum.

A century later, Peter the Great (1682–1721) devoted his formidable energies to, as he put it, 'opening a window onto the West'. He undertook extensive travels in western Europe, adopted western European dress, persuaded prominent western Europeans to come to Russia, and created his new capital at St Petersburg, the better to communicate with western Europe – though he did all this without surrendering an ounce of his native brutality.

Once Russia had learned about Europe, it was then Europe's turn to become acquainted with the Russian empire, now a player on the international scene, and impressive not only for its fearsome power but also with the mercurial nature of its rulers.

As Russia opened up to European influences, so – inevitably – did its fashions. Out went the hieratic robes hitherto worn by the tsarinas, and in came gowns copied from the latest Paris fashions, made in flowing, insubstantial fabrics that accentuated a more feminine silhouette. The same change could be observed in the jewels they wore: settings became more graceful and elegant, and massive cabochons gave way to sparkling diamonds. But any number of frills and furbelows à la Pompadour could do little to increase the charms – it has to be admitted – of the unprepossessing trio of tsarinas who reigned from Peter's death in 1725 to 1762: Catherine I, of stolid Lithuanian peasant stock, Anna Ivanovna, described as 'dull, coarse, fat, harsh and spiteful', and the wilful, capricious and astoundingly vain Elizabeth. None the less, the reputation of the Russian empire was sealed, and would endure down the centuries. The Russian Empire was the mightiest in the world and the most awe-inspiring, ruled over by tsars and tsarinas who were among the most cruel and extravagant, unpredictable and flamboyant sovereigns the world had ever seen. Their jewels, meanwhile, were to form the most fabulous collection in the world, exceeding in magnificence and scale even those of the princes of India and Persia. To the rest of the world, Russia became embodied in its tsars and tsarinas, and in their fabulous collection of gemstones, more dazzling and spectacular than their wildest imaginings.

12

A PORTAIT OF THE GRAND DUCHESS EKATERINA ALEXEIEVNA before she became known to the world as Catherine the Great. Although at this point still only the wife of the heir to the throne, she already had great plans for her future. On a red ribbon she wears the Order of St Catherine, conferred on her by the reigning empress Elizabeth Petrovna, but in her hand she holds only a fan: the sceptre, symbol of power, is not yet within her grasp. Her fine, intelligent features suggest the presence of a great intellect and extraordinary determination. *Painting by Georg Christoph Grooth, State Hermitage Museum, St Petersburg.*

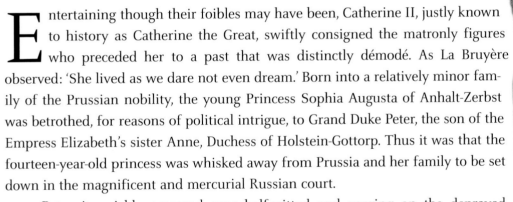

Catherine the Great *1762–1796*

Entertaining though their foibles may have been, Catherine II, justly known to history as Catherine the Great, swiftly consigned the matronly figures who preceded her to a past that was distinctly démodé. As La Bruyère observed: 'She lived as we dare not even dream.' Born into a relatively minor family of the Prussian nobility, the young Princess Sophia Augusta of Anhalt-Zerbst was betrothed, for reasons of political intrigue, to Grand Duke Peter, the son of the Empress Elizabeth's sister Anne, Duchess of Holstein-Gottorp. Thus it was that the fourteen-year-old princess was whisked away from Prussia and her family to be set down in the magnificent and mercurial Russian court.

Peter, it quickly emerged, was half-witted and verging on the depraved. Having changed her name to Catherine in order to be accepted by the Orthodox faith, the young princess quickly found her way into the favours of the reigning empress: her husband's unpredictable aunt, Elizabeth I. Though their relationship was a tempestuous one, involving incessant quarrels and mutual recriminations, Catherine clung on tenaciously throughout these years of uncertainty, when her fate hung constantly in the balance. Matters were eventually settled – though not in her favour – when Elizabeth died and her husband acceded to the throne, whereupon he immediately declared his intention of distancing himself from Catherine. Accustomed to spending drunken and dissolute evenings carousing with his officers, flaunting a mistress universally acknowledged to be strikingly ill favoured, and worshipping Prussia and all things Prussian, the new Peter III detested his wife.

Fearing at best divorce and at worst banishment to a convent or prison, Catherine displayed her characteristic resourcefulness. A plot to overthrow the Tsar was hatched, gathering strength and support among the army. One night Catherine slipped out of the imperial palace, changed into military uniform and – dashing on a white horse – assumed personal command of the rebel regiments. Her daring coup d'état succeeded, and it was her husband who was banished from the throne. Peter was imprisoned in a country house

SASH OF THE ORDER OF ST CATHERINE. Founded by Peter the Great in honour of his first wife, Catherine I, this order was conferred only on empresses, grand duchesses and other ladies of the highest rank. *Diamond Fund, Kremlin. Moscou.*

13

PENDANT OF THE ORDER OF ST CATHERINE, in diamonds and enamel on gold and silver (above). Late eighteenth century.

THE CORONATION REGALIA OF THE RUSSIAN TSARS. The great imperial crown, sceptre, orb, chain and star of the Order of St Andrew (opposite) are here displayed against the coronation mantle, in cloth of gold embroidered with the Russian imperial arms and edged with ermine. A few days after the assassination of her husband Peter III, Catherine summoned the Swiss jeweller Jérémie Pauzié and commissioned him to make a new set of coronation regalia, in a more modern style that was more appropriate for her reign. Pauzié selected the largest stones in the imperial treasury in order to meet Catherine's wishes. When he voiced his concern that the weight of the crown – five pounds – might be too much for the youthful Empress, she laughingly reassured him that, strengthened as she was by her new power, she wound find the crown light as a feather during the five hours of the coronation ceremony.
Diamond Fund, Moscow Kremlin

CATHERINE THE GREAT IN MOURNING DRESS (opposite) for Empress Elizabeth Petrovna, daughter of Peter the Great and last of the Romanovs. Elizabeth bequeathed the throne to her distant nephew, Peter III of Holstein-Gottorp, whose bride, the young German princess Sophie of Anhalt-Zerbst, was soon to become the celebrated Catherine II. Although she often suffered from the extremes of her volatile temperament, Catherine nevertheless felt a degree of affection towards the flamboyant Empress Elizabeth.
After a portrait by P. Rotari. Reproduced by kind permission of A La Vieille Russie, New York.

outside St Petersburg, and soon afterwards Catherine issued a proclamation announcing that he had died of a fit of colic. All Europe knew, however, that in fact Catherine's husband had been murdered by her lover, Grigori Orlov. All Europe was also convinced – although the truth would never be known for certain – that Catherine herself had ordered the murder.

Whatever the case, as Peter's widow and successor, Catherine found herself sole mistress of the world's largest and wealthiest empire. She relished her new power, which she exercised with complete autonomy and consummate skill. At once head of state, diplomat, politician and instinctive leader, she extended her empire, fostered progress in many spheres, and played a masterly game against rival powers.

This remarkably modern woman was the first to understand the importance of international opinion. Hence she cultivated the enlightened thinkers of the day, including great French writers such as Voltaire and Diderot, English philosophers and German poets, keeping up a sparkling correspondence with them and wooing them with magnificent gifts. So it was that she gained their approval of internal policies that ran to murder and even the occasional massacre when necessary. Any pretenders with serious claims to the throne, dragged from the dungeons in which they were already languishing, were the first to be unceremoniously dispatched. Merciless revenge was also to be the fate of Pugachev, a reckless impostor who claimed to be Peter III, and who escaped the murderous attentions of Orlov and Catherine to foment a popular uprising: he and his many supporters were indiscriminately put to death, with gallows erected in every village square.

Following the voracious tradition set by other tsarinas, Catherine boasted a long string of lovers. Among the most notable were Orlov, naturally, and also Prince Grigori Potemkin, the most outstanding of his successors, a larger-than-life figure like Catherine, and an indomitable soldier. The hot-headed and dishevelled Potemkin permitted himself unheard-of liberties with his imperial mistress, who turned a blind eye to his coarseness and adored him utterly. Together, Catherine the Great and Potemkin entered the ranks of the legendary love affairs of history.

EMERALD INTAGLIO DEPICTING CATHERINE II in profile, circled by diamonds and mounted in gold (above). The most friable of all precious stones, emeralds are notoriously difficult to engrave without shattering the stone. This piece therefore represents a technical tour de force.
Diamond Fund, Moscow Kremlin

17

MONOGRAM IN DIAMONDS OF CATHERINE (EKATERINA) II (above).
Jewels such as this were generally worn on the shoulder by the Empress's
ladies-in-waiting, signifying that they were in her service.

THE FUTURE PETER III AND HIS WIFE, THE FUTURE EMPRESS
CATHERINE II, with their Kalmuk (Mongol) pageboy (opposite). Beneath
the public show of affection, this was a couple consumed by mutual loathing.
Peter was abusive to Catherine, and as soon as he came to power repudiated
her, threatening to have her locked away in a convent. But before he had time
to put his plans into action he was usurped and assassinated, and Catherine
seized the throne in his place.
Painting by Anna Rosina Lisiewka, National Portrait Gallery,
Gripsholm Castle, Sweden.

PORTRAIT OF CATHERINE THE GREAT (opposite) by Vigilius
Eriksen (1778–1779). Resplendent in her coronation robes, the
Empress wears the imperial crown that had been made for her,
and holds the sceptre that was later to be set with the famous Orlov
diamond, and the new imperial orb, also commissioned for the
coronation. Around her throat is the imposing diamond necklace
of the Order of St Andrew. Her gown, of gold brocade embroidered
with double-headed eagles, is still preserved in the Kremlin. The
pomp and splendour of the coronation ceremony were the fruit of
years of preparation, and heralded the start of a reign of
corresponding magnificence.

In the eyes of posterity, Catherine the Great was to become the
very embodiment of Russia, and over the centuries that followed her
death she would become a symbol of totemic power for everything, great or small, touching upon the history of the Romanov
dynasty. An emblem of all things Russian and Romanov, she
would ensure the prosperity of all her Romanov descendants –
and perhaps all the more so since they were not in fact Romanovs.
Nor was Catherine herself, being born to a minor Prussian princely
family, and nor was her husband, for although his mother was the
daughter of Peter the Great, on his father's side Peter III was descended from the Holstein-Gottorp branch of the house of Oldenburg. Yet the
descendants of Catherine and Peter all bore the name of Romanov. The last tsar,
Nicholas II, would be assassinated under this patronymic, and to this day descendants
of the imperial family who escaped the Revolution claim it with pride. Only the Gotha
Almanac, in its scrupulous devotion to the truth, consistently refused to endow them with
the name of Romanov, listing the Russian imperial family under 'House of Holstein
Gottorp' – much to the indignation of successive tsars.

In the wake of the litany of scandals and mysterious disappearances that had marred
her reign, Catherine realized that the reputation of both her empire and her throne had
become tarnished and lacklustre. It was time to restore their glory, and she – a woman
ahead of her time, with an innate understanding of the importance of prestige and glamour – was the ruler to do it.

She set about building palaces and laying out gardens on a herculean scale, dwarf-
ing even the immense palaces constructed by her predecessor Elizabeth I. She enlarged the
Winter Palace and added the Hermitage, doubled the size of the gardens at Peterhof, and
at Tsarskoe Selo built a grandiose palace that remains to this day the largest in Europe.
Thus she created fitting settings for her legendary receptions, at which she demonstrated
an extraordinary ability to marry grace with majesty, and familiarity with firmness. All
who came into her presence seemed to fall under her spell, impressed not only by her
manner but also by her dazzling appearance. By nature Catherine appreciated simplicity,
and with advancing age she adopted a style of dress that was unadorned to the point of

BOUQUET OF FLOWERS
in white and coloured diamonds
and emeralds, mounted in gold and
silver (above). Brooches of this type
were known as *trembleuses*, as the
flowers were mounted on tiny
springs to ensure that they trembled
at the slightest movement, so
creating a lifelike impression.
Diamond Fund, Moscow Kremlin.

21

BROOCH IN SAPPHIRES AND DIAMONDS, mid-eighteenth century. The magnificence of the sapphires is enhanced by a setting of exceptional grace and elegance.
Diamond Fund, Moscow Kremlin.

austerity. But on state occasions she would always appear in gowns of the utmost elegance, in floating silks and satins, their billowing skirts emphasizing her small waist and their décolletages revealing her fine throat and shoulders. And on top of this she would take care to wear jewels of the utmost magnificence, very carefully chosen to emphasize her imperial power.

Although Catherine never wore jewels in private, they nevertheless exerted a powerful fascination over her. She set out to modernize the imperial insignia of power, commissioning a new crown made entirely of diamonds that nevertheless remained faithful to the traditional design, making reference to the quasi-religious status of the tsar. She had her new sceptre set with the enormous Orlov diamond, a gift from her lover, and commissioned an orb of gold set with diamonds and sapphires, unmistakably western in style. She bought quantities of paintings, furniture and cameos as well as precious stones and jewels. On state occasions she cut a dazzling figure, her corsage strewn with *trembleuse* brooches and other floral confections in diamonds, her skirts sewn with exquisite designs picked out with diamonds, and her powdered coiffure topped by the ravishing little diamond crown. Her wardrobe was governed throughout by the twin principles of good taste and magnificence.

In later life, as her figure thickened and grew heavier, she adopted an extremely simple style of dress, a sort of quilted robe topped by a cap. Behind the comfortable exterior of this benign-looking grandmother, however, lurked passions and appetites that continued unabated, requiring a supply of ever younger and more virile lovers. A formidable ruler feared throughout the world, a woman of magnetic attractions adored by strings of lovers, she nevertheless suffered an ignominious death on her commode. But posterity has drawn a veil over the excesses of the ageing Empress, remembering instead a Semiramis of the North, smiling and majestic, a graceful figure gliding through the great apartments of her palaces, the silk trains of her embroidered gowns rustling on the marble pavements and her toilette flashing with diamonds, trailing in her wake clouds of heady perfume and cohorts of admirers.

PORTRAIT OF CATHERINE THE GREAT in the uniform of the Preobazhensky Guards regiment (opposite), from the throne room of the palace of Tsarskoë Selo. As a reminder of the military support that had enabled her to seize power and keep a hold on it, the Empress was fond of wearing the uniform of certain regiments, and in particular of the Preobrazhensky Guards, who had played a key role in the coup d'état that had overthrown her husband Peter III.
Museum of Fine Art, Chartres, France.

THE POTEMKIN DIAMOND (above). This 50-carat diamond, cut from a raw diamond weighing 100 carats discovered in Brazil, was a gift to Catherine from her most celebrated lover, Prince Grigory Potemkin.
Reproduced by kind permission of Maison Kugel.

Page 26
PRINCE GREGORY ALEXANDROVICH POTEMKIN, a portrait painted in 1780 by an unknown hand. Though boorish, volatile and occasionally violent, in the eyes of his mistress Catherine the Great, the most powerful woman in the world, this incarnation of the red-blooded alpha male could do no wrong.
State Russian Museum, St Petersburg.

Page 27
STAR OF ST ANDREW in enameled gold set with diamonds. The Order of St Andrew was the Russian empire's highest decoration, reserved for its most illustrious subjects. Naturally Catherine bestowed it on her lover Potemkin.
Diamond Fund, Moscow Kremlin.

28

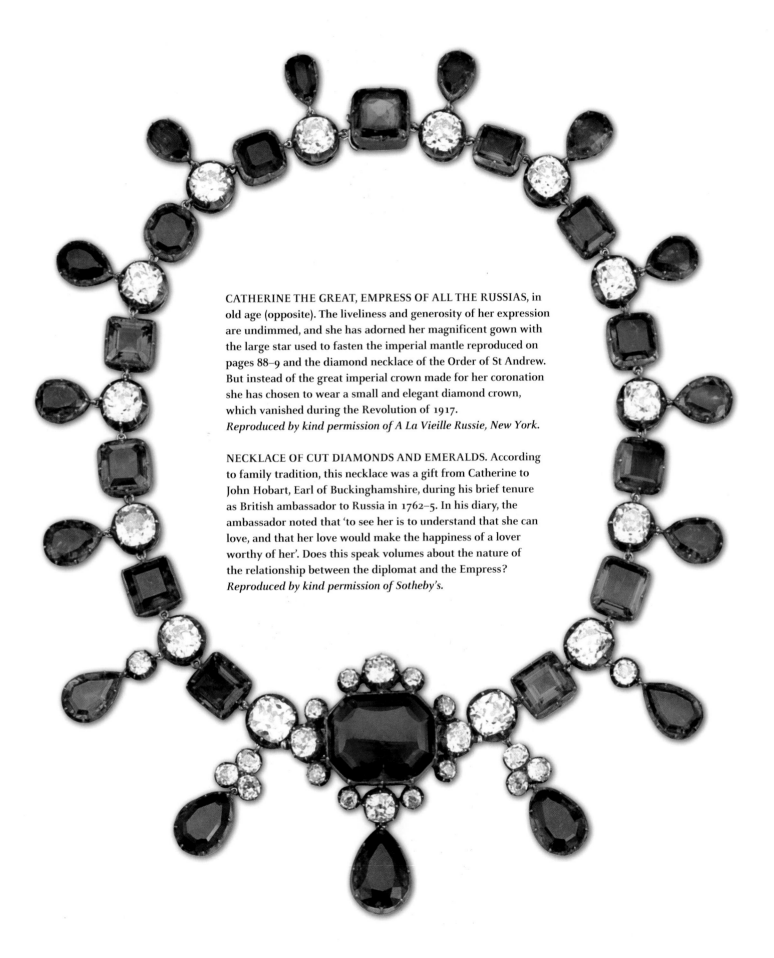

CATHERINE THE GREAT, EMPRESS OF ALL THE RUSSIAS, in old age (opposite). The liveliness and generosity of her expression are undimmed, and she has adorned her magnificent gown with the large star used to fasten the imperial mantle reproduced on pages 88–9 and the diamond necklace of the Order of St Andrew. But instead of the great imperial crown made for her coronation she has chosen to wear a small and elegant diamond crown, which vanished during the Revolution of 1917.
Reproduced by kind permission of A La Vieille Russie, New York.

NECKLACE OF CUT DIAMONDS AND EMERALDS. According to family tradition, this necklace was a gift from Catherine to John Hobart, Earl of Buckinghamshire, during his brief tenure as British ambassador to Russia in 1762–5. In his diary, the ambassador noted that 'to see her is to understand that she can love, and that her love would make the happiness of a lover worthy of her'. Does this speak volumes about the nature of the relationship between the diplomat and the Empress?
Reproduced by kind permission of Sotheby's.

Paul I *1796–1801*

Benevolent and beloved though she might have been as a grand-mother, as a mother Catherine the Great was truly monstrous. Perhaps she was ashamed of her only son: with his coarse features, grotesque snub nose and small, drooping eyes, and his person quite devoid of his mother's poise or majestic presence, Paul was ugly and awkward. Though intelligent enough he had little wit, and his upbringing had turned him into a haunted and wild-mannered recluse, inhabiting his own world of obsession, paranoia and fear.

Oppressed by the heavy burden he was forced to bear of a mother who enjoyed universal acclaim, he was also tormented by rumours of his own illegitimacy, to which Catherine herself lent credence in her memoirs. Without his mother's consent, moreover, he was not allowed to make the smallest decision or take any kind of initiative, however insignificant. Even when she presented him with a country house with the avowed intention of letting him furnish and decorate it to his own taste she was incapable of leaving him alone, making every decision herself, even down to the smallest details – and in the process creating the masterpiece that is the palace of Pavlovsk. Systematically humiliated, neglected and bullied, Paul became obsessed with thoughts of revenge.

At last, with his mother's death and his own accession to the throne, his time came. In the eyes of history and of most his contemporaries he was by now both dangerous and deluded, a Jekyll and Hyde character whose often brutal whims teetered on the brink of insanity. Capricious and demanding to a degree, he imposed outrageously harsh punishments for the most trivial and insignificant lapses, condemning those unfortunates who incurred his wrath through some minor transgression or other to be whipped or exiled to Siberia. Living in fear and dread under this reign of terror, his subjects could only look back with nostalgia to the golden days of his mother's reign. At the Tsar's approach everyone fled, not least members of his own family. It was whispered at court that he planned to remove the succession from Alexander, his eldest son whom he subjected to a constant

GRAND DUKE PAVEL PETROVICH, TSAREVICH (later Tsar Paul I). From the large number of reproductions of this famous portrait by Alexander Roslin, painted in 1777, we know that it was the only one for which Paul I ever sat. This complex, peculiar, unpredictable and unhappy ruler has been harshly judged by both his contemporaries and posterity. Yet his intelligence was in some respects remarkable, and some of his views were far in advance of his time. To this day his reputation as a madman ensures that he is venerated by many Russians.

31

BROOCH IN THE FORM OF A HAT, in emeralds, diamonds and rubies
mounted in gold (above). The eighteenth century saw fashions in jewellery,
which had hitherto been very rigid, assailed by original and surprising flights
of fancy, as in this sumptuous evocation of a stylish hat.
Diamond Fund, Moscow Kremlin.

GRAND DUCHESS AND FUTURE EMPRESS MARIA FEODOROVNA, wife
of Paul I (opposite). Following the death of his first wife, a princess of Hesse,
the future Paul I married a princess from a minor branch of the Württemburg
dynasty, known as the Montbéliard family after the French city over which they
ruled at that time. Although the couple had little in common and Paul was an
abusive and unfaithful husband, an unlikely but strong bond of affection
and even love grew up between them.
Anonymous. c.1800. Russia.

A PORTAIT OF PAUL I IN FULL IMPERIAL REGALIA (opposite). Paul wears the great imperial crown made for his mother and the chain of the Order of St Andrew, and holds the imperial sceptre. Standing in front of the throne (shown below), he also wears the tunic and insignia of the office of Grand Master of the Order of Malta. In order to thwart the ambitions of Napoleon, who had conquered Malta, Paul created a Russian Order of Malta, undeterred by the fact that in its origins this decoration was quintessentially Catholic.
By Vladimir Borowikowski, 1800. State Russian Museum, St Petersburg

IMPERIAL THRONE OF GILDED WOOD, surmounted by the imperial crown and upholstered in crimson velvet embroidered with the imperial arms (above). So pleased was Paul I with this design, by the court architect Vincenzo Brenna and executed by the court cabinetmaker Meier, that he commissioned no fewer than six copies of it. This one, placed in the throne room of his wife Maria Feodorovna, remained in use until the Revolution of 1917.

barrage of abuse, and that he was plotting to send his devoted wife Maria Feodorovna to a nunnery in order to put his mistress, Princess Galitzin, on the throne.

Yet, Paul I genuinely wanted the best for the Russian people, pushing through bold measures of reform and taking an interest in the lot of his humblest subjects. Though a cruel dictator he was also a reluctant autocrat, who sought to temper and transform the absolute powers of the imperial Russian throne. And although he did not know how to express his feelings, underneath his harsh exterior he was a family man, deeply and sincerely attached, despite all appearances to the contrary, to both his children and his wife.

His first marriage had been to a princess of Hesse-Darmstadt, who almost immediately after their wedding died, so slipping back into the complete obscurity whence she came. Subsequently Paul married the Württemberg princess who was to become Empress Maria Feodorovna. Every morning in Montbéliard, the small French town and possession of the Duke of Württemberg where she was born and brought up, she had heard the Württemberg royal march played, along with every other inhabitant of the place. These included one Rouget de Lisle, who when some years later he received a rush commission to compose music for La Marseillaise, looked no further than this anthem of a minor monarchy with which he was so familiar. In the intervening period, the princess had left this provincial backwater for the immense empire and sumptuous court over which she was to reign. Her love for her bizarre husband was as sincere as it was wholehearted, though his response was to accuse her of infidelity, and to her dying day she remained a tireless defender of his memory.

Like all German princesses, Maria Feodorovna had two great interests, genealogy and jewels, twin passions which were to be shared by all the Russian tsarinas (all of them German princesses) who followed her. In her youth, when she and her husband had visited France in the guise of the Comte and Comtesse du Nord and she had become friends with Marie-Antoinette, Maria Feodorovna had been quite pretty. But as the years passed so her waistline steadily expanded, until she appears in her portraits as a dauntingly matronly figure, ever more flamboyantly decked out in jewels until she began to resemble nothing more than a jeweller's shop window.

Not to be outshone, her husband also liked to be painted dripping with diamonds, and even his everyday regalia featured a massive solitaire diamond securing the pale blue ribbon of the order of St Andrew to his epaulette. In numerous portraits he is depicted sporting the imperial crown jewels, and especially the imperial crown made for his mother, which he liked to wear at a slightly jaunty angle as though it were a top hat.

Meanwhile, the momentous events of history seemed to be crowding in upon each other at a furious pace. In France, the Revolution had given way to Napoleon Bonaparte. So incensed was Paul I on learning that this Corsican upstart had captured the island of Malta that he declared himself Grand Master of the Russian Knights of Malta, regardless of the fact that this ancient order was a paragon of Catholic – rather than Russian –

GRAND DUCHESS ALEXANDRA PAVLOVNA. The little girl in this unattributed portrait (opposite), painted in the late 1790s, also happened to be Grand Duchess Alexandra Pavlovna, daughter of the Emperor of all the Russias, and so – despite her tender years – she is encumbered with a pearl necklace, opulent earrings and an imposing diamond-encrusted diadem. Later she would marry Archduke Joseph of Austria, in one of the very few unions between an Orthodox bride and a Catholic groom.
Anonymous. c.1790. State Hermitage Museum, St Petersburg.

orthodoxy. Once a crown of the order had been made for him, topped by the famous Maltese cross, he lost no time in having his portrait painted in his new role as Grand Master.

Now this most unpredictable of men, consumed hitherto by a burning hatred of both the Revolution and Napoleon, abruptly changed his mind and fell into the arms of the First Consul – a reversal greeted with dismay by England, the motivating power and focus of all resistance to the French. The reaction of Paul I, whose tendency to suspect hostile conspiracies and intrigues on all sides was not without foundation, was to build a new palace that was at once a fortress and barracks in the middle of St Petersburg. Hardly was the Mikhailovsky Palace completed than he incarcerated himself inside and raised the five drawbridges that were the sole means of crossing its moat. Here was one place where he at last felt safe.

A mere week later, this was the place where he was brutally assassinated by a group of courtiers whom he considered among his most loyal and dependable friends. 'Another English coup!', cried the First Consul when he heard the news.

Persuaded by the conspirators that his father was plotting to have him killed, Paul's eldest son, Alexander, had given his backing to a coup d'état, but not to an assassination.

TIARA OF BRILLIANTS (above). This jewel, one of the most sumptuous in the personal collection of the tsarinas, was destined to be one of the very few to survive the Revolution. At its centre is a 10-carat pink diamond of exceptional quality and value, bought by Paul I. This tiara was a favourite of the last tsarina, Alexandra Feodorovna, wife of Nicholas II. *Diamond Fund, Moscow Kremlin.*

GRAND DUCHESS AND FUTURE EMPRESS MARIA FEODOROVNA, wife of Paul I (opposite). This portrait shows the Grand Duchess at the period when she and her husband undertook a grand tour of France, travelling incognito under the pseudonyms of the Comte and Comtesse du Nord. They were received with great ceremony and affection at the court of Versailles, where Maria Feodorovna and Marie-Antoinette laid the foundations of a firm friendship. *By Alexander Roslin.*
State Hermitage Museum, St Petersburg.

SOUVENIR CASE in gold, mother of pearl and enamel (left), embellished with a miniature portrait of a lady of the imperial family, probably one of Paul I's daughters. The rise of sentimentalism in the late eighteenth century saw the production of increasing numbers of such 'tokens of friendship', including objects of considerable value.
Diamond Fund. Moscow Kremlin.

BROOCH IN THE FORM OF THREE MARGUERITES in yellow and white diamonds (right), with the stem and leaves in gold and green enamel.
Diamond Fund. Moscow Kremlin.

From the floor below he had heard everything. Knowing the awful truth, he flatly refused to succeed his father under such conditions.

At this point the imposing figure of his mother Maria Feodorovna appeared, wailing and dishevelled. Invoking the examples of Catherine I and Catherine II, both of whom had reigned without husbands, she demanded the right to succeed her husband to the throne. Unceremoniously pushing her aside, the conspirators – most of whom were blind drunk – dragged her son by force to the Winter Palace, where against his will and with their speech slurred by drink they proclaimed him Tsar of all the Russias. Such was the general relief at the removal of Paul I that no objections were raised.

The Russian people did not forget Paul so quickly, however. With the native understanding inbred in them for centuries they were shrewder judges of his true nature than many men of power and influence. So it is that to this day, and virtually alone among the pantheon of the tsars, his tomb is always decorated with fresh flowers. During the Soviet era, the official version was that the Russian people had an innate respect for madmen. Today's guides explain that he was a good man who was loved by the people.

Europe was scandalized by the mysterious deaths of too many tsars in too quick succession, attributed to fits of apoplexy or colic in which nobody believed. Wits remarked that the young Alexander I rode to his coronation preceded by the men who had murdered his grandfather, escorted by the men who had murdered his father, and followed by the men who would happily murder him. To which Count Münster, Hanoverian envoy to St Petersburg, famously added the view that the Russian constitution rested on 'absolutism tempered by assassination'.

39

GRAND DUCHESSES ALEXANDRA AND ELENA PAVLOVNA, daughters of Paul I (above). Alexandra would later marry Archduke Joseph of Austria, while Elena would wed Prince Friedrich Ludwig of Mecklenburg-Schwerin. The daunting Tsar was a loving father, who was held in deep affection by his children, and especially by his daughters. Bizarre and unfathomable though he may have been, Paul I none the less succeeded in creating an unusually close family.
By Elisabeth Vigée-Lebrun.
State Hermitage Museum, St Petersburg.

CAMEO IN RED AND WHITE AGATE on a grey background, ringed by diamonds (above). The late eighteenth century witnessed a renaissance in the ancient Greek and Roman art of cameos; in Russia these tended to depict members of the imperial family in classical Greek costume, as in this example with its border of large diamonds.
Diamond Fund. Moscow Kremlin.

CHOKER AND EARRINGS in the form of garlands of roses with bees gathering nectar (opposite). The blooms and insects are formed from cut white, yellow and orange diamonds, and together they form a unique and priceless ensemble. The leaves are of gold and green enamel.
Diamond Fund. Moscow Kremlin.

Pages 42–43
THE OLD MIKHAILOVSKY PALACE IN ST PETERSBURG, was built by Paul I towards the end of his reign. Convinced he was under threat from numerous conspiracies, the Tsar was determined to seek safety in a fortress of his own design. No sooner was this great citadel finished than he incarcerated himself within it, only to meet his death a short time later at the hands of a group of his most trusted courtiers. His brutal assassination took place in his apartments on the first floor of the left-hand wing. This engraving of the palace depicts a military review in front of the main entrance, under the lofty gaze of an immense equestrian statue of Peter the Great.

ALEXANDER I (opposite). At barely twenty years old, the newly crowned Tsar Alexander I was already the darling of the empire and would soon be the idol of all Europe. Handsome, generous and open-minded, he liked to think of himself as a liberal. Though he affected a simplicity in his dress and demeanour, the pin on his ermine cloak is of rubies and diamonds. Behind the confidence of his youthful smile he seems haunted by anxiety: compromised from the outset by his father's assassination, his reign was to prove a stormy one.

Alexander I *1801–1825*

Tall and slim, with a fine figure, gentle blue eyes and a delicate complexion, Alexander I was generally considered to be an Adonis among men. Indisputably a ladies' man, in both his character and his attitudes he also demonstrated an indefinable feminine quality. One his most beguiling traits was his desire to dispense with pomp and ceremony, encouraging his subjects to overlook the fact that he was the most powerful sovereign on earth and treat him as just an ordinary man like any other. Nobody was fooled by this unconventional approach, needless to say, but to many it proved irresistibly appealing. The true nature of the intelligent man who lay behind this seductive exterior was to remain an enigma, an act of dissimulation that over the ensuing years was to metamorphose into an instinct for survival.

This was the age of Napoleon, who bestrode Europe like a colossus and established his presence even in Russia. Soon Europe looked on with bated breath as Alexander, this inexperienced young man, squared up to the great and unstoppable conqueror. The outcome of this duel to the death was only too easy to predict, and all sympathies lay with the hapless Alexander. Yet it rapidly became clear to Napoleon that he could neither completely overcome by force nor completely seduce by blandishments the young Tsar, whom in a fit of pique he dismissed contemptuously as 'this shifty Byzantine'.

In the end, after one of the most remorseless campaigns in history, it was the Byzantine who emerged victorious, aided by his innate gift for dissimulation allied to dogged determination. But he would never have won without the wily and typically Russian genius of his commander in

MINIATURE OF ALEXANDER I (above), encircled by diamonds and mounted on a ring. The originality of this jewel lies in the bezel covering the miniature, which is itself a specially cut diamond.
Reproduced by kind permission of S. J. Phillips Ltd., London.

SASH OF THE ORDER OF ST ALEXANDER NEVSKY (left). After the Order of St Andrew, this was most illustrious of all Russian orders, founded by Peter the Great. Russian decorations were not only the most numerous but also – and by a long way – the most sumptuous in Europe. The star is in diamonds and enamel mounted in gold and silver.
Diamond Fund. Moscow Kremlin.

45

**BRACELET IN GOLD AND ENAMEL WITH A MINIATURE OF
ALEXANDER I.** The Gothic-inspired design of this piece (opposite)
is ahead of its time, anticipating by some twenty years the vogue for the
Gothic Revival style. As with the ring shown on the previous page,
the miniature is 'glazed' with a bezel cut from a 25-carat diamond.
Diamond Fund, Moscow Kremlin.

chief General Kutuzov, and perhaps most of all without the
overwhelming force of his most faithful ally 'General Winter',
the terrible and merciless Russian cold that was to annihilate the
Grande Armée as it retreated from the burning city of Moscow.
Thus this smiling, self-effacing young man found himself hailed
as the conqueror of the seemingly invincible Napoleon and the
liberator of Europe.

In the years before the French invasion of Russia, when France and
Russia were bound by a treaty of friendship, Napoleon had asked for the hand
of one of Alexander's sisters in marriage. With instinctive revulsion, Alexander
had instructed his mother to reply that she was unwilling to part with her
daughters. To be doubly sure of avoiding the kind of matrimonial snares that
seemed to be set with such rapidity and frequency wherever Napoleon was
concerned, the sisters were hurriedly married off to German princelings.

The tables were turned, however, when Alexander sought to marry one of
them to the Duc de Berry, heir presumptive to the French throne. Now it was
his turn to receive an uncompromising rebuttal from Louis XVIII: although
at this time he cut a far from impressive figure and the French royal family
was sorely in need of a few well-chosen dynastic marriages to restore its dig-
nity and standing, the head of the Maison de France deemed that these upstart
Romanovs were bold to the point of impudence in presuming to seek an alliance
with his nephew. Alexander's victories notwithstanding, among the ruling dynasties of
Europe the Romanov dynasty had yet to earn its spurs.

In his pursuit of Napoleon, meanwhile, Alexander led his troops beyond the
empire's western frontier and on across Europe to Paris itself, which he entered to wild
acclaim. It was an episode that left fond memories on both sides, one of the most endur-
ing being the introduction into the French language of the Russian word *bistrot*, meaning
'quickly', which the Parisians heard on the lips of hungry Cossacks and took as an
urgent plea for food. But with the celebrations came fear and anxiety: in European eyes,
Alexander I was rapidly turning from a free-thinking liberator to an insatiable ogre, determined to swallow up a large part of Europe. His charm to the fore, the young Tsar succeeded in allaying – for the moment at least – this new and negative image of Russia.

Back at the Russian court, simplicity was the watchword during his reign. The dazzling jewels and huge gemstones adored by his forebears were anathema to Alexander I,
whose most ostentatious gift was a ring bearing his portrait in miniature, protected by a
diamond bezel. He had married Princess Marie of Baden, one of the greatest beauties of
her time and, as Empress Elizabeth Feodorovna, the most ravishing of all the tsarinas. It

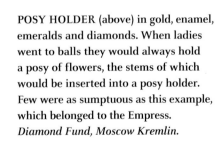

POSY HOLDER (above) in gold, enamel,
emeralds and diamonds. When ladies
went to balls they would always hold
a posy of flowers, the stems of which
would be inserted into a posy holder.
Few were as sumptuous as this example,
which belonged to the Empress.
Diamond Fund, Moscow Kremlin.

EMPRESS ELIZABETH FEODOROVNA, wife of Alexander I, by Elisabeth Vigée-Lebrun (opposite). Though she was considered a beauty, her husband sadly proved immune to the attractions of the former Princess Marie of Baden, and took a string of mistresses. She in turn found consolation in the arms of lovers. Yet shortly before his death, which still remains shrouded in mystery, Alexander and Elizabeth enjoyed a period of genuine reconciliation.
Private collection, New York.

BOX IN VERMEIL AND MAUVE ENAMEL (above) bearing the imperial emblem of the double-headed eagle, symbolizing the tsars' dual powers, both spiritual and temporal. The orb is a baroque pearl, and the sceptre is set with rubies.
Diamond Fund, Moscow Kremlin.

was not long, however, before Alexander was seduced by the charms of the Polish Madame Naryshkina; deeply hurt, the Tsarina eventually found consolation in the arms of Adam Czartoryski, prince of the most illustrious Polish family and a fervent patriot. Leaving the magnificent jewels worn by earlier tsarinas in their caskets, she preferred to appear in her portraits dressed in a style of unadorned elegance, the very model of the graceful simplicity brought into vogue by her husband.

The same was true of Alexander's sisters, in whose portraits no elaborate jewels are allowed to distract from the beauty of their figures, often revealed by plunging décolletages. Alexandra was the only Romanov to marry a Catholic, a Habsburg prince; then came Elena, Anna and Maria, who married the Grand Duke of Saxe-Weimar and became an enlightened patron of the arts and protector of Franz Liszt. But Alexander's favourite sister was always Catherine – so much so, indeed, that the word 'incest' was heard on the lips of more than one courtier. Brother and sister loved nothing more than to embark on wild and almost unaccompanied expeditions through the countries of a Europe newly liberated from the Bonapartist yoke, galloping along roads still churned up by the war. In London, where no expense had been spared in preparing a magnificent reception for them, they outraged the Prince Regent with the coarseness of their behaviour.

Still there were no jewels to be glimpsed at the Russian court. In the aftermath of a long and crippling war, simplicity was as much a necessity as a matter of taste. The grip of austerity was further hardened by the influence of Madame de Krüdener, a former adventuress who had turned to religious mysticism of a muscular nature, founding what would now be known as a cult. Falling under her spell, Alexander renounced – for her sake and for God's – his chivalrous ways and romantic dalliances. Encouraging him to look into his soul and his conscience, the mystic effected a reconciliation with his beautiful Tsarina. Together he and Elizabeth set off, in dead of winter, for the sake of her health, on a journey to a small village in the Crimea.

There, miles from anywhere, Alexander fell ill, and a few days later died. But did he really die? Over the following decades rumours grew that he had staged his own death in order spend the rest of his life as a hermit in Siberia, in expiation of his indirect part in the assassination of his father Paul I. Recent studies seem to confirm these rumours. The alluring ruler and handsome conqueror lived on for many years as a man of God, bearded and devoid of worldly goods, in a snowbound blockhouse in the middle of the Siberian wilderness: proof, if proof were needed, of the altogether singular nature of the Romanov dynasty.

TIARA OF AMETHYSTS AND DIAMONDS, which may also be worn as a necklace (above). These amethysts, the finest in the world, came from Siberian mines owned by Alexander I. Smitten by the charms of Anne, Marchioness of Londonderry, the bashful Tsar offered her this gift as a token of his love. Lady Londonderry contrived to emerge from this imbroglio, as she termed it, with blameless innocence, her honour – and her amethysts – intact. The tiara remains in her family to this day.

    The Russian imperial jewels were not merely decorative, but also served as a propaganda weapon for the tsars, their unrivalled magnificence standing as an emblem for the formidable might of the Russian empire. Thus as well as being worn by the tsarinas and grand duchesses, they were also bestowed by the tsar with lavish magnificence on other ladies of distinction.
Collection of the Marquess of Londonderry.

A SUMPTUOUS PARURE OF EMERALDS AND DIAMONDS (opposite), another gift to the beautiful Anne, Marchioness of Londonderry, from Alexander I.
Collection of the Marquess of Londonderry.

GRAND DUCHESS CATHERINE PAVLOVNA (opposite). A piquant beauty
with something of the Kalmuk features of her father Paul I, portrayed at a
period when simplicity was in vogue, and the dazzling imperial jewels
remained locked away in their caskets. Alexander I was inseparable from his
favourite sister, causing much speculation at court about the nature of their
relationship. Catherine was married first to a Prince of Oldenburg and then to
the King of Württemberg, before her death at the age of only thirty-one.

A CHRYSOLITE WEIGHING 193 CARATS (above), ringed by 30 brilliants
and mounted as a pendant. Chrysolite means 'golden stone' in Greek, and this
lovely olive-green stone – more commonly known by the name of peridot –
gives off a golden glow.
Diamond Fund, Moscow Kremlin.

PAIR OF EARRINGS IN SAPPHIRES AND DIAMONDS, matching the brooch shown on page 23. These glorious earrings, made in the late eighteenth century, were worn by every tsarina until the Revolution of 1917. Having seized power, the Bolsheviks found themselves in urgent need of cash, and so they resolved to sell off all the imperial jewels. Then, influenced by Trotsky, they decided to preserve a few pieces of historic value, such as the crowns and a few personal jewels. These earrings are therefore one of the rare examples of Revolutionary taste to have survived the tragic events of the period intact. *Diamond Fund, Moscow Kremlin.*

BEDCHAMBER OF GRAND DUCHESS ALEXANDRA FEODOROVNA
in the Anitchkov Palace. Standing on Nevski Prospekt in St Petersburg,
the Anitchkov Palace was the residence of the heir to the Russian throne.
It was here that Grand Duke Nicholas, brother of Alexander I, lived
before acceding to the throne with his wife Alexandra.

Most of the numerous and immense imperial palaces were the
property of the crown. Members of the imperial family were financed in
lavish fashion by revenues from the imperial estates – some millions of
acres of agricultural land and forest – distributed among them by the
tsar. Thus their sumptuous way of life was assured, and they were able
to maintain the palaces placed at their disposal.

The grand room depicted in this watercolour by Edward Hau
illustrates the triumph of the Empire style that prevailed during the
reign of Alexander I, with draperies in the antique style, obelisks,
classical Roman urns, and torchères and lamps of classical inspiration.

57

NICHOLAS I AT PETERHOF (oppposite). A military man to the core of his being, Nicholas I was rarely seen out of uniform, even in this 'holiday' setting in front of the 'cottage' at Peterhof, painted by Igor Bottmann in 1849. Forsaking the vast halls and endless corridors of the imperial summer palace, Nicholas and Alexandra had a comparatively modest villa built in the grounds, which to them felt like a proper family home. In the background, warships are shown patrolling the Baltic.
By Igor Bottmann. 1849.

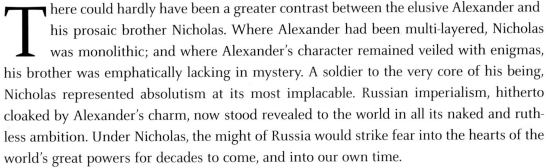

Nicholas I *1825–1855*

There could hardly have been a greater contrast between the elusive Alexander and his prosaic brother Nicholas. Where Alexander had been multi-layered, Nicholas was monolithic; and where Alexander's character remained veiled with enigmas, his brother was emphatically lacking in mystery. A soldier to the very core of his being, Nicholas represented absolutism at its most implacable. Russian imperialism, hitherto cloaked by Alexander's charm, now stood revealed to the world in all its naked and ruthless ambition. Under Nicholas, the might of Russia would strike fear into the hearts of the world's great powers for decades to come, and into our own time.

In 1839 the Marquis de Custine, a Frenchman forced to leave his country after a homosexual scandal, travelled through Russia, where he proved a shrewd and perceptive observer of people and society. The world that emerges from his informed reflections and brilliant *apercus*, later published as *Letters from Russia*, remains instantly recognizable to this day, with its pettifogging, narrow-minded bureaucracy, its ubiquitous secret police, and its gulags, of which everyone knew but no one spoke. But in the absolute authority and undeniable grandeur of Nicholas I's regime there was also a certain panache. This devout patriot and arch conservative, the avowed champion of authoritarianism in its most despotic form, was nevertheless extremely fond of his sister-in-law, Grand Duchess Elena, wife of the Tsar's brother, described in glowing terms in his *Memoirs from Beyond the Grave* by the arch snob Chateaubriand, who met her in Rome.

The Grand Duchess was a prominent liberal and free-thinker, who at her salons in her immense residence, the Mikhailovsky Palace, openly received intellectuals who in the view of the authorities were among the most dangerous and deeply suspect in the empire. Nicholas remained undeterred, and in his frequent visits to the Grand Duchess listened to her views while reserving his own, so demonstrating an unexpected capacity for open-mindedness. Generally speaking, however, Nicholas had nothing but contempt for anyone who was not either a Romanov or closely connected to the dynasty, and this attitude was to imbue his fellow Romanovs and their descendants. With a tsar whose ambition was to conquer the planet at their head, the Romanovs became convinced that their dynasty was uniquely illustrious and distinguished. It was under the influence of Nicholas that the

PAIR OF EARRINGS in diamonds and red spinels (above). At this period, no distinction was made between rubies and the slightly less valuable red spinels. Thus in the imperial inventory, these earrings are described as being set with rubies. Dating from the mid-eighteenth century, they were worn by every tsarina in turn.
Diamond Fund, Moscow Kremlin.

EMPRESS ALEXANDRA FEODOROVNA, wife of Nicholas I (opposite). Princess Charlotte of Prussia, daughter of Friedrich Wilhelm III and the incomparable Queen Louise, embraced the Orthodox religion and changed her name on her marriage to the heir to the Russian throne. Once he had come to power, her fanatically nationalistic husband encouraged her to wear costumes inspired by Russian history. In this portrait after Franz Krüger she is wearing the archaic dress of three centuries earlier, her kokoshnik or traditional headdress, bodice and jewels set with rubies of colossal size, all of which have today vanished without trace. Hardly less impressive than the rubies are the pearls of her necklace and the diamonds strewn throughout her ensemble.
Reproduced by kind permission of Sotheby's.

BROOCH set with a square-cut emerald of 137 carats, surrounded by diamonds (above). The Russian imperial court was renowned not only for the quality of the jewels in its treasury, but also for their sheer size. Stones of exceptional proportions from mines in the Russian Urals, Brazil, India, Burma and Ceylon all made the long journey to Russia.
Diamond Fund, Moscow Kremlin.

BROOCH set with a sapphire of 260 carats, surrounded by diamonds (above right).
Diamond Fund, Moscow Kremlin.

Romanov grand dukes, and most of all the grand duchesses, began to display the inimitable hauteur that was to become their hallmark among the long-suffering royal families of Europe. However illustrious the courts in which they found themselves, and contrary to all established protocol, these daughters and sisters of the Russian tsars invariably expected to be accorded precedence over all other crowned heads.

Nicholas I had married Princess Charlotte of Prussia, one of the daughters of the famous Queen Louise, who had been received in the Orthodox faith and now reined as Empress Alexandra Feodorovna. Tall, angular, elegant and majestic, she displayed both character and courage. Her husband had numerous affairs, and it was even rumoured that one of these peccadilloes had involved him indirectly in the duel that was to prove fatal to the most celebrated subject of his empire, the poet Pushkin. But throughout these amorous adventures he retained a deep attachment for the Tsarina, always according her the utmost respect and unlimited funds.

For her part, Alexandra Feodorovna perfectly understood what Nicholas sought to achieve, and she made sure that she presided over a court that became a byword for glittering magnificence. The German in her found it impossible to refrain from imposing a degree of order on ceremonies and celebrations that hitherto had been characterized by a typically Russian form of chaos. She increased the ranks of court officials, appointing numerous chamberlains and ladies in waiting, all resplendent in dazzling costumes; and

TIARA OF PEARLS AND DIAMONDS (opposite) made for Empress Alexandra Feodorovna, wife of Nicholas I, by the Swedish jeweler Bolin in 1841. In fact this photograph shows an exact replica of this piece, made by Soviet jewelers. The original was sold after the Revolution, when it was bought by the Duke of Marlborough for his wife Gladys, who later sold it in her turn. On this occasion it was bought by Imelda Marcos, in whose collection it remains.
Diamon Fund. Moscow Kremlin.

GRAND DUCHESS ELENA PAVLOVNA, née Princess Charlotte of Württemberg, wife of Grand Duke Mikhail Pavlovich, painted with her daughter Maria by Karl Briullov in 1830 (below). The brilliant and highly cultivated princess held court to a salon of writers, musicians and artists at her residence, the vast Mikhailovsky Palace, now the State Russian Museum. Unapologetically liberal in her views, she lent her support to the democratic movements and left-wing intellectuals of the day. Yet her brother-in-law Nicholas I, a despot to his enemies and widely acknowledged as rigidly and implacably authoritarian, not only failed to forbid contact with Grand Duchess Elena but also listened attentively to her views and held her in great esteem. She is shown here with her young daughter Grand Duchess Maria, who was to die unmarried at the age of twenty-one.
State Russian Museum, St Petersburg.

she threw open the imperial residences – the Winter Palace, Tsarskoë Selo and Peterhof – where she gave balls of overwhelming opulence for up to six thousand guests. Setting out single-mindedly to impress, she succeeded admirably: foreign visitors returned to their countries with breathless accounts of awe-inspiring splendour, and even Indian maharajahs were forced to admit that they had never seen such a wealth of jewels, nor stones of such superlative quality. The Tsarina fully understood the power of jewels, and all who had been guests at her court bore witness to its unparalleled magnificence

Alexandra Feodorovna brought the imperial jewels out of store, unlocking jewel caskets and safes that had remained firmly closed for many years, and – like the other ladies of the imperial family – literally covered herself in a profusion of colossal gemstones as though it were the most natural thing in the world. She had her bedchamber lined with tailor-made cabinets in which she displayed her personal jewels: one cabinet for diamonds, one for pearls, one for sapphires, one for rubies, one for emeralds, and so on. Altogether there were some twenty of these cabinets, covering the walls from floor to ceiling and all filled to overflowing with jewels.

Under Nicholas I, the grand duchesses were elevated to the status of demi-goddesses. Whenever they entered into marriage alliances with foreign powers, with great sovereigns or princes, their overriding duty was to retain their Russian identity. The Tsar ensured that they left the Russian court armed with monumental dowries and jewelry collections such as never before been seen in the West. When Anna Pavlovna, the Tsar's favourite sister who had married to become Queen of the Netherlands, lost her jewels in a fire that destroyed her newly built palace, Nicholas promptly replaced them all with exact replicas. To this day, the presence of a Romanov ancestor in the family tree of any of the royal families of Europe, impoverished or otherwise, may reliably be deduced from the size of their jewels.

Nicholas's daughter Alexandra had scarcely had time to arrive in Germany to marry a prince of the Hesse-Kassel family before she expired. Yet to this day the descendants of that family may be seen sporting the remnants of her massive dowry. Her sister Olga

63

GRAND DUCHESSES OLGA AND VERA KONSTANTINOVNA, granddaughters of Nicholas I: miniature portraits (below) painted by C. Lallemand in 1856. With their demure poses and their simple coral necklaces, their imperial highnesses indicate the dawn of a new spirit of simplicity, and perhaps even a hint of democratization within the imperial family.
Private collection, Paris.

CROWN OF THE TSARINAS (opposite), entirely encrusted with diamonds, some of them of considerable size. During the coronation ceremony, the tsar himself would place the great imperial crown on his own head, before crowning his wife as she knelt at his feet. This crown was made for the coronation in 1801 of the first wife of Paul I, Elizabeth of Hesse.
Diamond Fund, Moscow Kremlin.

Nikolaievna, who became Queen of Württemberg, endowed her new family with a sapphire the size of a hen's egg and a sash some two metres (six feet) long encrusted with diamonds. Olga was the apotheosis of these glorious creatures, superbly beautiful, gracious yet aloof, and imperial to the tips of their elegant fingers, who would make their appearance at the head of a sweeping staircase or at the lofty doors to a sumptuous ballroom. Their white throats would be encircled by ten rows of pearls and their coiffures topped by tiaras of imposing dimensions and set with gemstones of peerless quality. To these would be added heavy earrings cascading down to their shoulders, diamond bracelets, a generous scattering of brooches on their sumptuous gowns, and even shoe buckles encrusted with rubies and emeralds. The artist Ferdinand Bac, seeing Queen Olga Nikolaievna drive past, escorted by horseguards in colourful uniforms, was struck by 'her extraordinary presence, at once benevolent and glacial.'

But the Tsar's favourite daughter was Olga's elder sister, the intellectually brilliant Grand Duchess Maria Nikolaievna. In order to keep her near him in Russia, he married her off to a German princeling – a Beauharnais on one side and hence a descendant of the Empress Josephine – who declared that he was only too delighted to make his home in Russia. After his death she fell in love with a Count Strogonov and married him in secret, never daring to tell her father, whose reaction she could predict only too well. Nicholas I would have been outraged at a Romanov marrying a simple aristocrat, and a Russian to boot. Thus Maria Nikolaievna lived in perfect happiness, keeping a secret that was known to all except her father.

Nicholas I's brand of despotic, aggressive imperialism was bound ultimtely to provoke a reaction from the powers of Europe. In 1854, on the pretext of defending the Ottoman empire, Britain, France and Austria – united for once – joined forces in attacking the Crimea, inflicting a terrible defeat on the woefully ill-equipped and poorly supplied Russian army. Within months of this humiliation, Nicholas I was dead.

A MEDIEVAL CARROUSEL AT TSARSKOË SELO (opposite), organized by special command of Nicholas I in 1843. Horace Vernet's painting shows the Tsar with Empress Alexandra Feodorovna and their children in troubadour-style medieval costumes. To the left of the imperial couple, the Tsarevich Alexander and their son-in-law Duke Maximilian of Leuchtenberg are depicted on horseback, while Grand Dukes Constantine, Nicholas and Michael are dressed up as pages. Grand Duchesses Olga and Alexandra, meanwhile, are draped in velvets and brocades. Their eldest sister, Grand Duchess Maria, does not appear in the painting as she was busy receiving and entertaining courtiers who had been invited to the Alexander Palace.
On exhibition at the Alexander Palace, Tsarskoë Selo.

Page 68
GRAND DUCHESS OLGA NIKOLAIEVNA, wife of Ludwig I, King of Württemberg. Inordinately proud of her Russian imperial blood, Grand Duchess Olga was described by a contemporary observer as 'at once benevolent and glacial'. Lest anyone should forget that she was the daughter and sister of tsars, she has festooned herself in jewels from head to toe, even to the point of having enormous pearls sewn on to her train and the ribbons on her skirts.

page 69
THREE BOWS IN DIAMONDS mounted in gold and silver, created by Jérémie Pauzié, jeweller to Catherine the Great, who made the coronation regalia to her command.
Diamond Fund, Moscow Kremlin.

BROOCH IN DIAMONDS AND RED SPINELS (above), matching the earrings shown on page 59. This brooch, set with stones of outstanding quality, was made in 1760 for Empress Elizabeth I, the last of the Romanovs. It was also a favourite with the tsarinas who followed her.
Diamond Fund, Moscow Kremlin.

PORTRAIT OF EMPRESS ALEXANDRA FEODOROVNA, wife of Nicholas I, by Christina Robertson (opposite). Here the wife of the world's most powerful sovereign leaves us in no doubt as to her wealth and prestige: the sapphires of her brooch are huge, and her rope of pearls must measure several metres in length. A woman of courage, intelligence and humanity, Alexandra was the heart and soul of her family and presided over the most sumptuous court in Europe.

THE 'FERME' AT PETERHOF (right) provided a haven of simplicity for Nicholas I and his family from the suffocating pomp and protocol of the never-ending round of official ceremonial at court. Turning their backs on the lofty apartments of the palace of Peterhof, the imperial couple preferred to accommodate their family in the comparatively confined space of a modest villa they had built in the palace grounds. This watercolour by Edward Hau shows them driving out in a carriage drawn by a single horse, led by a mujik. Amid all the privilege, wealth and prestige that surrounded them, the imperial family at this time chose to lead a daily life of surprising simplicity.

page 74
GRAND DUCHESS MARIA NIKOLAIEVNA was the eldest and favourite daughter of Nicholas I. She shared his strength of character and natural authority, but in addition was an intellectual of great cultivation and a patron of the arts. Refusing to countenance her ever leaving Russia, her father married her off to a German princeling who was prepared to live in St Petersburg. The residence chosen for the couple was the Mariinsky Palace, nowadays home to the St Petersburg Legislature. For years she was the mistress of Count Stroganov, in a long-term and happy relationship that was common knowledge to everybody in the empire except her father. They had had several children together, and eventually, after the deaths of both her first husband and her father, she married him. In this portrait by T. A. Neff, the Grand Duchess wears only a few jewels, but those mostly of exceptional size: the pear-shaped pearls of her necklace, the cabochons of her brooch and the veil studded with tiny pearls that covers her head all indicate her illustrious rank.

page 75
PINK TOURMALINE OF 226 CARATS, cut in the form of a raspberry and mounted in gold and green enamel. In addition to their numerous parures of the most precious stones, such as diamonds, sapphires, rubies and emeralds, the tsarinas also boasted parures of semi-precious stones such as tourmalines, aquamarines, amethysts, peridots, topazes and others.
Diamond Fund, Moscow Kremlin.

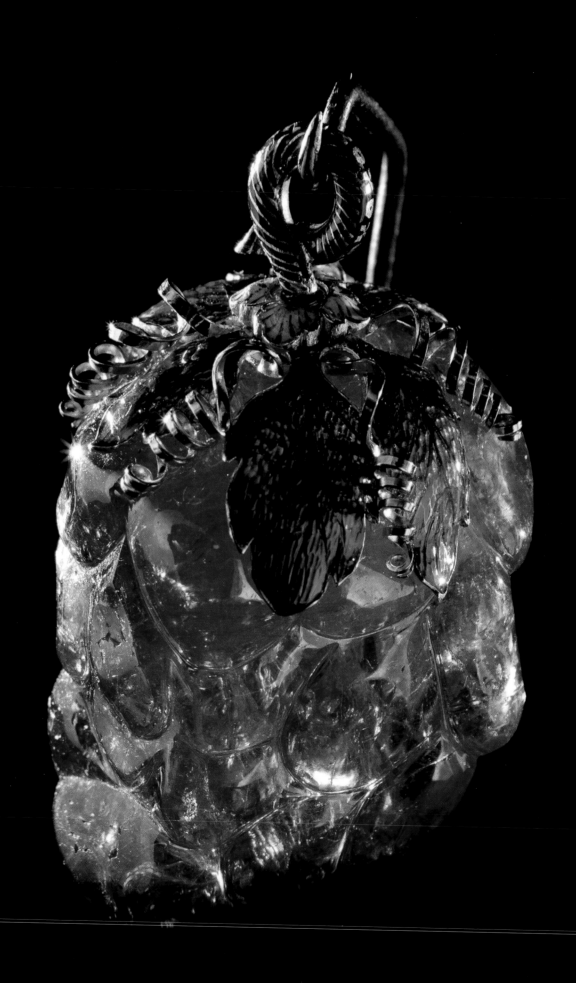

EMPRESS ALEXANDRA FEODOROVNA'S STUDY in the Anitchkov Palace, which she used during the time before the Tsarevich Nicholas acceded to the throne. Born Princess Charlotte of Prussia, the Empress had been brought up in Berlin, and the decoration of this intimate room recalls the Prussian palaces of her childhood. Typically of the fashions of the 1830s, a variety of outstanding *objets d'art*, such as the marble vases on the mantelpiece, the classical vase in the foreground and some paintings, jostle with a clutter of undistinguished bric-à-brac chosen for comfort rather than for any aesthetic qualities. Luigi Premazzi's watercolour faithfully reproduces the pot plants, family souvenirs, mahogany furniture, chintz armchairs and inevitable piano, de rigueur for amateur musical entertainments, that crowd the space. Already the bourgeois taste that was to become so widespread under the influence of Queen Victoria is starting to encroach on imperial – and quintessentially unbourgeois – Russia. In the ceiling, meanwhile, the grandeur of the Empire style remains undimmed.

Alexander II *1855–1881*

The antithesis of his despotic and unyielding father, Nicholas I, Alexander II never-theless did not share the easy charm of his uncle Alexander I. The new Tsar's passion was for ideas: a confirmed liberal in his views, he was intelligent and open-minded, to a degree that some considered rash. Realizing that sooner or late absolutism was doomed, he made it his mission to open Russia up to the western world and its ideas, and to bestow upon the empire institutions worthy of a democracy. Among the most far-reaching and controversial changes enacted by the 'Tsar-Liberator' was the abolition of serfdom, and on the very morning of his horrific assassination he had given his assent to a document outlining the first steps towards parliamentary rule.

Tall, handsome, and universally acknowledged to be exceptionally agreeable com-pany, the future Tsar had demonstrated his democratic spirit early on, when he had been dispatched by his parents to find a bride among the apparently inexhaustible supply of German princesses. He got no further than Darmstadt, home of the eldest daughter of the Grand Duke of Hesse, who had been allotted a prominent place on his list. It was with her younger sister Marie that he fell in love, however, declaring to his parents: 'She it is or nobody.' At this news his parents were thrown into a state of acute confusion: how could they break it to their son that the ravishing Marie was beyond doubt illegitimate, the fruit of an illicit liaison between the Grand Duchess and a Swiss colonel, and that even the Grand Duke had been forced to recognize that she had been born out of wedlock? Sublimely undeterred, Alexander promptly declared that if he had to renounce the suc-cession in order to marry Marie he would willingly do so. To the astonishment of all

BROOCH OF DIAMONDS AND RUBIES mounted in gold and silver (above). Of an unusual shape, it was designed to be worn on the ceremonial cap of the Order of St Catherine. *Diamond Fund. Moscow Kremlin.*

79

EMPRESS MARIA ALEXANDROVNA, wife of Alexander II, painted by Franz Xaver Winterhalter in 1857 (opposite). As heir apparent to the Russian throne, the young Alexander had been sent on a tour of the German courts in quest of a suitable bride. One of the candidates on his list had been the eldest daughter of the Grand Duke of Hesse-Darmstadt, but it was her younger sister Marie who captured his heart. His parents were opposed to the match and refused to be won over, but Alexander was adamant, and in the face of his determination they at last yielded. Alexander had triumphed against almost universal opposition, and yet despite all expectations the marriage did not prove a happy one. Alexander fell for the charms of the young Catherine Dolgoruky, conducting an ostentatious affair with her while Maria Alexandrovna suffered a slow death from tuberculosis.

concerned his parents relented, indicating another slight and unexpected chink in Nicholas I's otherwise reactionary and autocratic armour. On her arrival in Russia, the young princess melted all hearts with her delicate beauty and natural grace.

Liberal though he was, Alexander II expected his court to be every bit as magnificent as his father's. Two great beauties presided over it: Empress Maria Alexandrovna, and her sister-in-law Grand Duchess Alexandra Josefovna, both of whom were immortalized in portraits by Winterhalter. The Empress is depicted amid a cascade of pearls, with ropes twining through her hair and streaming down to below her waist. Photographs of Alexandra Josefovna, meanwhile, show her sporting quantities of enormous sapphire or emerald cabochons surrounded by almost equally enormous diamonds. The rest of the imperial ladies presented an equally dazzling spectacle, festooned with jewels commissioned from the finest jewelers in Paris, Germany, Sweden, and of course Russia.

Having created a sensation with his single-minded pursuit of Maria Alexandrovna, Alexander proceeded to neglect his wife in favour of the young Princess Catherine Mikhailovna Dolgoruky, who was just nineteen (to his forty-seven) when he declared his passionate love for her. Hopelessly smitten, Alexander whisked Catherine away with him on the pretext of visiting the Exposition Universelle in Paris, and even when they were both in the same city bombarded her with love letters: six thousand of them in a period of only a few years. Together they had three charming children, and their relationship was no secret from anyone, least of all the unhappy Empress. Unlike Maria Alexandrovna, Katia, as the Tsar called her, wore no jewels: her natural beauty needed no adornment, and to prove it she was bold enough to have her portrait painted in the nude.

Rejuvenated by this relationship, Alexander applied himself to affairs of state with renewed zeal, drawing up a constitution with his favourite brother, Grand Duke Constantine, and General Loris-Melikov, an Armenian whom he had appointed as his chief minister.

Though now suffering from consumption to add to her woes, and obliged increasingly to withdraw to her private apartments, the Empress none the less made it a point of honour to maintain her court at the highest pitch of extravagance. The last and most lavish ceremony over which she presided was to be the marriage of her only daughter, Maria

pages 82–3
THE CORONATION OF ALEXANDER II in the Cathedral of the Assumption in the Kremlin. The Tsar, already crowned, now crowns his wife, Maria Alexandrovna. On his right stands his mother, the Empress Mother Alexandra Feodorovna; in the foreground are the imperial ladies-in-waiting. This coloured engraving taken from the coronation souvenir album captures the profusion of hieratic images of saints on the walls and columns of the cathedral, the thousands of candles, the clouds of incense, the glittering brocaded robes of the bearded prelates, and the slow and fascinating rituals of the coronation ceremony, imbued with Orthodox mysticism – all of which plunged western visitors into the fabulous world of a distant and thrillingly oriental past.
Reproduced by kind permission of Sotheby's.

DIAMOND BROOCHES (left) in the form of a basket of
flowers, second half of the eighteenth century.
Diamond Fund, Moscow Kremlin.

Alexandrovna, to Prince Alfred, Duke of Edinburgh and second son of Queen Victoria. Victoria entertained a deep and suspicious antipathy towards Russia, fuelled by the awareness that it was the only rival that posed any real threat to the British Empire, and took a dim view of the union. At this time, she and the Tsar between them possessed over half the world. The American mistress of one of the Russian grand dukes has left a description of the breathtaking splendour of the wedding celebrations: the vast salon lit by countless candles; the immense ballroom thronged with guests and shimmering with jewels and gold embroidery; the monumental silver platters and dishes; the breathtaking floral arrangements; and the supper tables laden with the rarest and costliest delicacies, transported by special train from every corner of the empire and even Europe. The American lady was particularly lost in admiration before the appearance of the imperial ladies, in brocade gowns of every shade – rose pink, pastel blue, soft yellow, almond green – trimmed with filmy gold and silver gauze, gossamer-fine lace, chinchilla and sable, and adorned above all by glittering cascades of every conceivable gemstone, set in jewels of every imaginable form.

The bride, decked out in a suite of rubies and diamonds given to her by her father, wore a sullen air throughout, while her tottering mother, weakened by illness, was literally bent under the weight of her innumerable diamonds, each of them the size of a hazelnut.

Maria Alexandrovna was to survive a few years yet, and even as she lay in her death agony she was taunted by the sounds of her rival's children capering in the rooms above her. Within weeks of her funeral, Alexander caused a scandal by marrying his Katia, talking openly of his intention of crowning her and bestowing the title of grand duke on their sons. Another draft constitution was prepared, to the chagrin of left-wing activists, mostly of anarchist or nihilist tendency, whose propaganda it undermined. The controversial Tsar-Liberator, who in his later years had swung against the liberalism of his youth, had been the victim of numerous unsuccessful assassination attempts, mostly from the left. Tragically it was at this point, just as he seemed to be reaching a point of real achievement in both his personal and his political life, that the Tsar was blown apart by a hand grenade tossed into his path by a terrorist.

Dreadfully mutilated, Alexander was carried back to the Winter Palace, leaving a trail of blood in the snow. There he was laid on a couch in his study to die, when Katia burst in, clad only in lacy deshabille, and flung herself upon his bloody remains, crying out his pet name, 'Sasha!' The imperial family was profoundly shocked by this exhibition. Unabashed, she retired in glory that very day, conducting herself like the empress she believed herself to be. She died in exile in Nice after the Revolution of 1917, old, tyrannical and impoverished.

NECKLACE AND TIARA IN RUBIES AND DIAMONDS (above), created by
the Swedish jeweler to the imperial court, Bolin. The necklace is of resolutely
modern design; the design of the tiara is based on four-leaved clovers. Together
they were a gift from Alexander II to his daughter, Grand Duchess Maria
Alexandrovna, on her marriage to Queen Victoria's second son, Alfred, Duke
of Edinburgh. The Grand Duchess's excessive pride in her imperial birth were
to cause innumerable upsets and considerable friction at the English court,
particularly with her formidable mother-in-law. The laws of succession meant
that she and her husband were also to inherit the titles of Grand Duke and
Grand Duchess of Saxe-Coburg-Gotha. Maria Alexandrovna survived the
Russian Revolution and the First World War, to die of a heart attack when
(the story goes) to her horror she found herself being addressed by the new
German authorities as 'Frau Coburg'.
Reproduced by kind permission of Sotheby's.

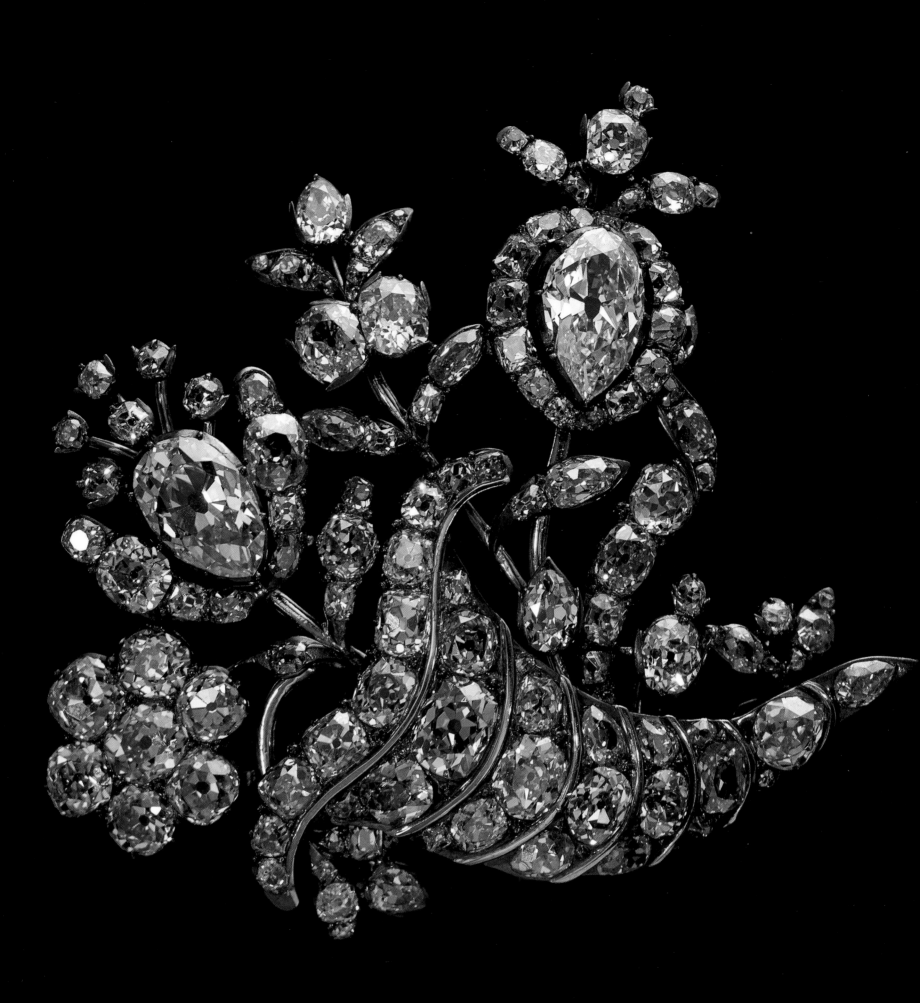

Page 86

Page 86
ALEXANDRA OF SAXE-ALTENBURG, GRAND DUCHESS
KONSTANTIN, by Franz Xaver Winterhalter. This celebrated
beauty married the favourite brother of Alexander II, whose
liberal views had a considerable influence on him. Proud of
her figure, the Grand Duchess used to keep her corsets on at
night in order to preserve her wasp-like waist, and had silver
and ivory paper knives made in the charming shape of her
foot. Rather than decking herself out from head to toe in jewels
to sit for this famous German portrait painter, the Grand
Duchess has chosen to wear only a simple string of pearls,
knowing full well that her personal beauty far outshone all
the treasures of the imperial court. It did not, however, prevent
her husband from establishing a second household with an
actress, by whom he had numerous children.

page 87
HAIRPIN IN DIAMONDS mounted in gold, in the form of
a cornucopia, created in 1781 by Louis David Duval, a French
jeweller who worked at the Russian court during the reign
of Catherine the Great.
Diamond Fund, Moscow Kremlin.

FASTENING-PIN OF THE IMPERIAL MANTLE (opposite).
Composed of a multitude of diamonds, most of them coloured
and unequal in size, this jewel was made in 1750 for the
coronation of Tsarina Elizabeth I, daughter of Peter the Great and
the last of the Romanovs. From that time on, it was used to
fasten the long mantle of cloth of gold, embroidered with double-
headed eagles and edged with ermine, worn by the tsars at their
coronation and by imperial brides on their wedding day.
Diamond Fund, Moscow Kremlin.

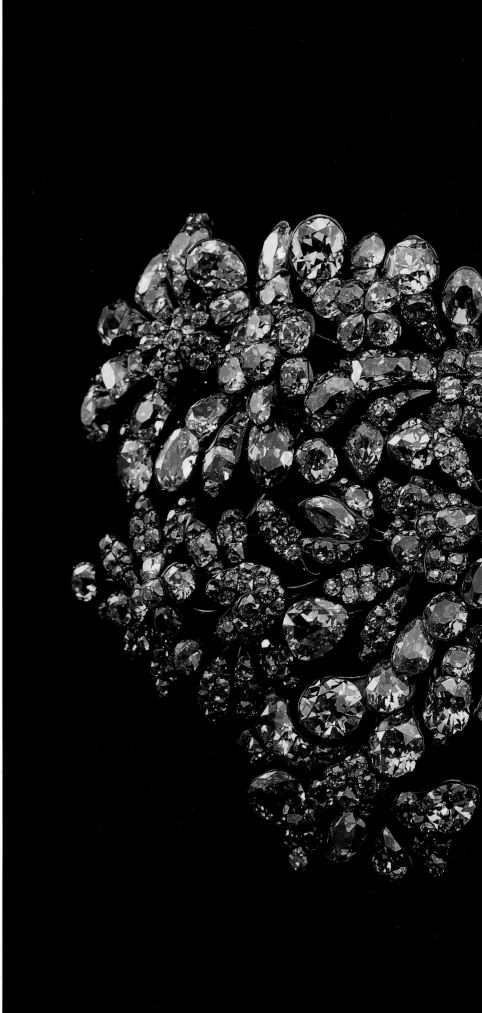

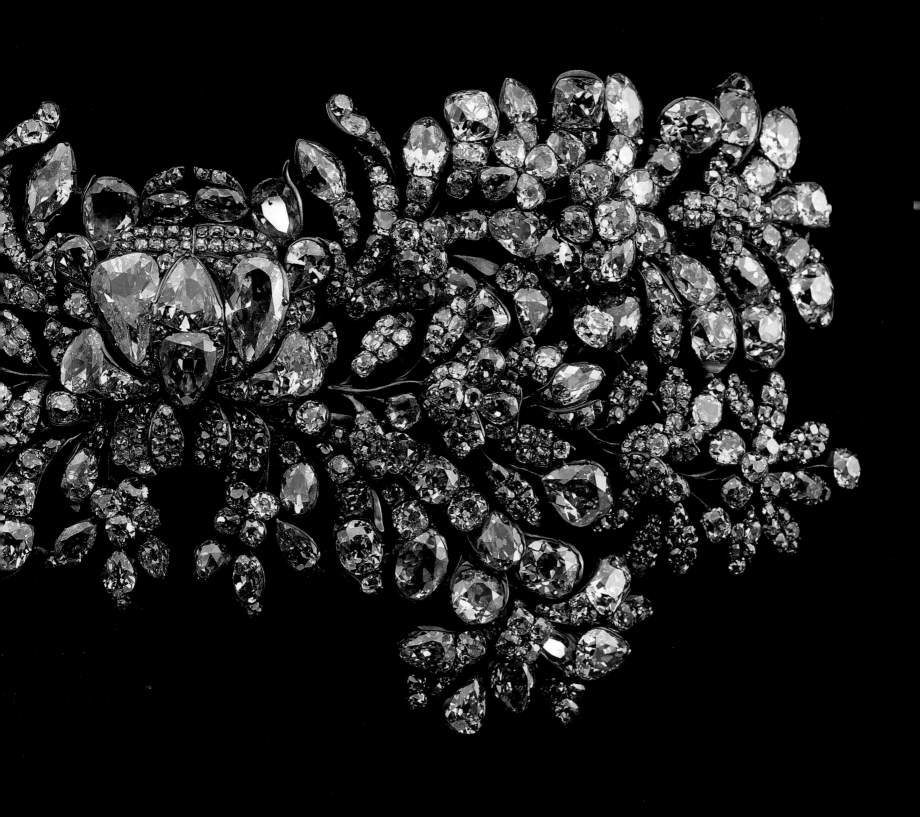

NECKLACE OF DIAMONDS (above), mounted in gold and silver, from the collection of Catherine the Great. Originally a trimming sewn on to one of the Empress's ceremonial evening gowns, this piece was among the crown jewels sold off by the Bolsheviks. It subsequently passed through several hands, before coming up for sale at Sotheby's Geneva. The bow in diamonds and silver is a later addition.
Reproduced by kind permission of Sotheby's.

CATHERINE MIKHAILOVNA DOLGORUKY (opposite). Born in 1847, Catherine became the mistress of Alexander II in 1866 and had three children by him. A few months after the death of Empress Maria Alexandrovna in 1880, the Tsar married her, giving her the title Princess Yurievska. A year later he was assassinated. Princess Yurievska survived the Revolution and died in poverty in Nice in 1925.
Private collection, Nice.

FOUR DIAMOND PINS (opposite). The pair in the form of spirals of diamonds mounted in gold and silver, are hatpins; the other two are cravat pins, one set with a 7-carat blue diamond and the other with a 3.36-carat pink diamond. Diamonds are found in a wide of range of colours, but these two stones in the most popular and sought-after colours today are both extremely rare and of outstanding quality.
Diamond Fund. Moscow Kremlin.

EARRINGS IN EMERALDS AND DIAMONDS (above). The imperial treasury contained an extraordinary number of unmounted stones, many of which were secretly sold by Nicholas II in 1905 to cover the deficit caused by the Russo-Japanese war. During the reign of Alexander II, by contrast, the treasury was filled to overflowing. These superlative cabochon emeralds were a gift from him to his daughter-in-law Maria Pavlovna on the occasion of her marriage to his son Vladimir. Later they were surrounded with diamonds and worn as earrings by Maria Pavlovna's granddaughter, Princess Olga of Yugoslavia.
Reproduced by kind permission of Sotheby's.

93

GRAND DUCHESS MARIA ALEXANDROVNA on a childhood excursion
(above) in the grounds of Tsarskoë Selo in 1858. Alexander II's only daughter,
Maria Alexandrovna was also his favourite child. Two footmen hold the bridle
of the pony drawing the little girl's carriage, a valet walks behind, and a lady-in-
waiting leans over her solicitously, all ready to obey her smallest whim. In the
background of this watercolour by F. Feichel, 1858 is the Alexander Palace.

EGRET BROOCH (opposite) in Brazilian diamonds and natural pearls, late
eighteenth century.
Reproduced by kind permission of A La Vieille Russie, New York.

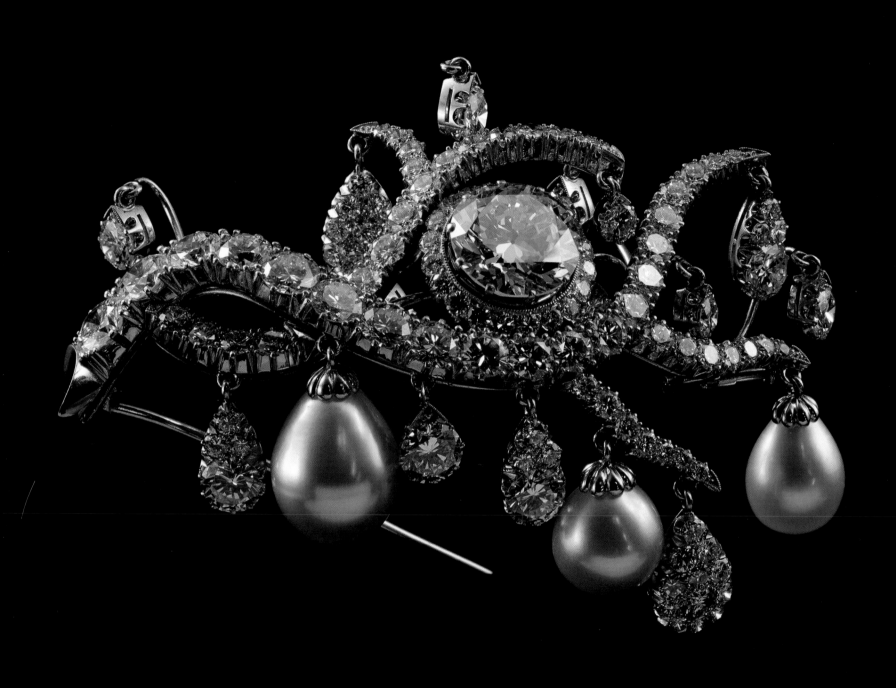

THE THRONE ROOM IN THE WINTER PALACE, ST PETERSBURG.
Designed in the eighteenth century by the architect Rastrelli, the
Throne Room became the setting for the most stirring of imperial
events. With its glittering chandeliers and imposing colonnades,
this magnificent chamber reflected all the grandeur of the empire.
The throne shown here was a replica of the one illustrated on page
34. It was in this room that the Duma was inaugurated in 1905.
Colour lithograph, 1855. Pushkin Museum, Moscow.

ALEXANDER III, his wife Empress Maria Feodorovna and their son, Grand Duke George, by Tuxens (opposite). Born Princess Dagmar of Denmark, Maria Feodorovna had initially been betrothed to Alexander's elder brother Nicholas, who died suddenly at the age of twenty-one. Equally suddenly redundant, Dagmar was rapidly re-betrothed to his younger brother, now heir to the throne. Despite its ill-omened beginnings, the marriage was to prove a great success, with Alexander and his wife remaining devoted to each other throughout their married life. Grand Duke George, their second son, was to die of consumption before reaching adulthood.
National History Museum, Frederiksborg Castle, Denmark.

Alexander III *1881–1894*

Alexander III was a giant of a man, a colossus possessed of legendary physical strength. Within that great frame, however, there lurked an intellect that was abnormally small. Narrow-minded, dull-witted, stubborn as a mule, he put an abrupt and violent end to his father's tentative moves towards representative government – tearing up the unsigned document left on his desk – and announced an instant return to absolutism in its most extreme and intractable form. Xenophobic to a degree, he coined the watchword 'Russia for the Russians'. He decreed that Russian was henceforth the only language to be spoken at court, and his detestation of Queen Victoria – equalled only by her detestation of himself – put paid to the vogue for all things English. But at the same time this patriotic fervour drove him to found the Russian Museum, dedicated to the commemoration of Russia's glorious past. Under his iron rule, the new Tsar was confident of renewed glory for his empire, to continue for centuries to come.

As it had never been anticipated that Alexander would succeed his father, he was singularly unprepared. But his elder brother Nicholas, who with his intelligence and fine sensibilities was everything that Alexander was not, had died prematurely at the age of twenty-two, following an illness according to some sources, or a mysterious accident according to others. Before his untimely death he had been betrothed to Princess Dagmar of Denmark; the question then arose, what was to be done with his fiancée? There was a cold logic about the proposed solution: the obvious answer was for her to marry Nicholas's younger brother and the new heir to the throne. Yet the docile Dagmar apparently accepted this arrangement without question. One of the many children of the impoverished Prince Christian of Schleswig-Holstein-Sonderborg-Glucksburg, she had enjoyed a carefree though frugal upbringing during which the girls had learned to patch and mend their own dresses. The death of King Frederick VII without an heir, however, was to catapult Christian out of obscurity and onto the Danish throne where, as Christian IX, he became not only father to the future Kings of Denmark and Greece, but also grandfather to the King of Norway, and father-in-law to the Tsar of Russia and the King of England. It was an extraordinary reversal of fortune that he accepted with his customary natural and unaffected simplicity.

KEEPSAKE BROOCH in diamonds and pearls (above), set with miniatures of Alexander III and his wife Maria Feodorovna, *née* Princess Dagmar of Denmark. This brooch, created by Bolin for Alexander III's coronation, was a gift from the Tsar to his mother-in-law, Queen Louise of Denmark. It remains in the Danish royal collection.

CENTREPIECE OF THE CHAIN OF THE ORDER OF ST ANDREW, in gold, enamel and diamonds. This jewel was worn by the tsars at their coronation. *Diamond Fund, Moscow Kremlin.*

As Empress Maria Feodorovna, his second daughter was to display considerable force of character, allied with an understanding nature and a good deal of shrewd intelligence. With her petite figure she seemed the perfect complement to her great bear of a husband, to whom she was devoted. Once again, a huge gulf yawned between public opinion of the Tsar, which saw him as an odious oppressor, and his private reputation as an adoring husband and father and doting uncle. In the intimacy of his family circle, and especially among the many imperial children, the Tsar's feigned frowns and stern rebukes would provoke only squeals of delight.

The only matter over which Alexander III and Maria Feodorovna disagreed was court life. Gauche and awkward in company, the Tsar hated society occasions and parties, preferring quiet evenings at home with his family in the palace of Gatchina, outside St Petersburg. Maria Feodorovna, by contrast, was an incomparable hostess with an insatiable passion for grand dinners, balls and dances, and it was she who won the day. But balls with guest lists running to thousands were held less frequently, and the emphasis fell more on select parties with a mere few hundred guests dancing the night away.

Numerous awe-struck guests have left descriptions of the unforgettable entrance, announced by the court high chamberlain, that the Tsarina would always make on these occasions. Though less beautiful than her sister Princess Alexandra of England, she appeared more graceful, combining the dignified bearing of a sovereign with a feminine coquettishness. As the entire company dropped deep bows and curtsies, she would perform the three curtseys that court protocol demanded with celebrated poise. She dressed with an elegance that was as individual as it was stylish, taking her inspiration from the fashions of northern Europe rather than Paris. And throughout the day, from breakfast to supper, she would wear magnificent jewels with careless grace, a great cabochon sapphire with a pear-shaped diamond, and solitaire diamond earrings. For particularly grand occasions she favoured a necklace of peerless quality, featuring three rows of huge round-cut diamonds and a fourth row of even more dazzling pear-shaped diamonds. The inventory of the Tsarina's jewels at this time beggars belief.

Maria Feodorovna's only serious rival at court was the wife of Grand Duke Vladimir, Maria Pavlovna. This redoubtable German princess combined an in-depth knowledge of

EMPRESS MARIA FEODOROVNA, wife of Alexander III, *née* Princess Dagmar of Denmark. This painting (opposite) by the great German portrait painter Heinrich von Angeli, famous for his celebrated portrait of Queen Victoria, depicts the Empress as a picture of elegance in blue. The sumptuous pendant of pearls and diamonds that she wears was part of what she called her 'everyday jewels'. As she took these everywhere with her, they survived the Revolution. Her daughters later sold the pendant, which ended up in the collection of Lady Detterding, wife of the oil magnate Henry Detterding.
Private collection, Paris.

SNUFFBOX in gold and enamel (above), bearing on its lid a miniature of Alexander III beneath the imperial crown, surrounded by flowers and foliage in diamonds. Costly items such as this were commissioned in large numbers, to be presented by the tsar to retiring ambassadors or others who had distinguished themselves in his service.
Diamond Fund. Moscow Kremlin.

politics with an explosive personality and boundless ambition. At her salons in her palace on the Neva she cultivated everyone who was anyone within the Russian Empire, never failing to invite any distinguished visitors from abroad. In short, she was a force to be reckoned with. Wisely, and in the knowledge that even if they deployed their full arsenal of underhand tactics neither of them would emerge victorious, these two formidable women decided that their most prudent course was one of mutual cooperation.

Maria Pavlovna's great passion, even greater than her love of gowns, was for jewels, and her collection was even more fabulous than that of any other member of the imperial family, including the Tsarina herself. Her favourite occupation was shopping for magnificent gemstones and sending them to be set by Cartier or Chaumet, becoming one of their best clients. Her collection of emeralds was without equal, and she was also very fond of sapphires, in addition to the more usual diamonds and pearls. Photographs of her in all her finery are virtually a catalogue of the Russian imperial jewels.

The Tsar's happy home life and harsh reign were both doomed to come to an end, however. In 1888, the imperial train bringing Alexander III and his family home from the Crimea derailed, possibly as a result of a terrorist attack. The imperial family was taking luncheon in the dining car, the roof of which caved in, and it was only through the superhuman efforts of the Tsar, who supported the buckled carriage with his bare hands, that they escaped injury or death. His health was never fully to recover from the strain of that terrible day, however, and in 1894, aged fifty, he died of kidney failure.

THE GREAT IMPERIAL CROWN OF RUSSIA (opposite). Made for Catherine the Great for her coronation in 1762, the crown takes an unusual form, very different from other European crowns and first used by Peter the Great for his own crown. Peter had taken his inspiration in turn from the reclusive Holy Roman Emperor Rudoph II, who had devised a mitre-crown symbolizing the dual nature of the imperial power, embracing both the spiritual and the temporal. Catherine the Great's crown, probably the most sumptuous ever made, is encrusted with 4,936 diamonds and rows of magnificent pearls, surmounted above all by the red spinel of Peter the Great. Here the crown is flanked by the imperial sceptre and orb.
Diamond Fund, Moscow Kremlin.

Page 106
GRAND DUCHESS OLGA KONSTANTINOVA. The numerous granddaughters and great nieces of the tsars formed a bevy of young beauties. Just fifteen when this unattributed portrait was painted, Grand Duchess Olga Konstantinova is nevertheless extremely poised in her impressive pearls. Soon after this, a young Danish prince who had just become King George I of Greece arrived at the imperial court and fell under Olga's spell. He married her and took her to Athens, where she enjoyed great popularity as Queen of Greece.
Reproduced by kind permission of the Benaki Museum, Athens.

Page 107
ORDER OF THE GOLDEN FLEECE, in gold, diamonds and pink topazes. This chivalric order, inspired by the quest of Jason and the Argonauts in Greek mythology, was created in the Middle Ages by Philip the Good, Duke of Burgundy, and afterwards inherited by the kings of Spain and the Holy Roman Emperors. At this period it was customary for sovereigns to exchange their most precious decorations. Thus the Tsar sent the Order of St Andrew to the Holy Roman Emperor, who responded with the Order of the Golden Fleece. This highly coveted decoration, reserved for the most illustrious figures, evolved into a jewel of the highest value, set with diamonds and other precious stones.
Diamond Fund. Moscow Kremlin.

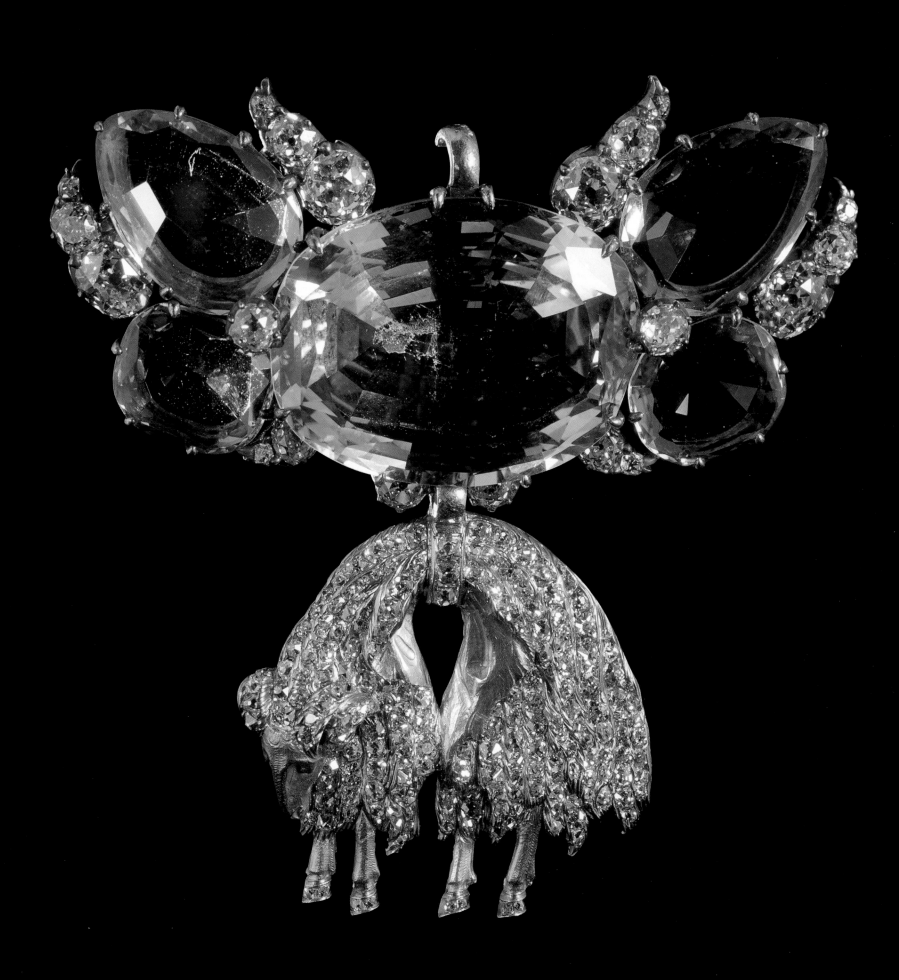

FOUR BROOCHES IN THE FORM OF INSECTS, made for the Russian imperial court in the years 1880–90 by the Swedish jeweler Bolin. These jewels of highly innovative design are faithful imitations of insects executed in stones of exceptional quality. The thorax of a cockchafer is formed by a baroque pearl, the tail of a dragonfly is encrusted with emeralds, and the wings of a butterfly are evoked in diamonds and sapphires. In their form and their originality, these brooches marry bold design with lyrical grace. *Diamond Fund. Moscow Kremlin.*

page 110
MARIA FEODOROVNA, wife of the future Tsar Alexander III.
With her many brothers and sisters, Princess Dagmar had been
brought up in relatively straitened circumstances, learning with
her sister Alexandra how to patch and mend their clothes. Then
Alexandra became Princess of Wales and finally Queen of England,
their father acceded to the Danish throne, and Dagmar became
Maria Feodorovna, future Empress of all the Russias.
Photograph by Georg Hansen, 1867, Copenhagen.

page 111
GRAND DUCHESS ANASTASIA MIKHAILOVNA, wife of Grand
Duke Friedrich Franz III of Mecklenburg-Schwerin (previous page,
left). The daughter of Grand Duke Mikhail and granddaughter of
Nicholas I is depicted wearing the traditional dress of ladies of
the Russian imperial court, with magnificent pearls, emeralds
and diamonds. It is hard to believe that this demure young girl
with such an air of innocence would lead such a turbulent life and
leave a lasting legacy of scandalous memories on the Côte d'Azur,
where she spent the last years of her life.

EMPRESS MARIA FEODOROVNA (previous page, right). During
the reign of her husband Alexander III, Maria Feodorovna started
the tradition of costume balls at which the imperial family and
members of the court would dress up as Russian nobles of the
sixteenth and seventeenth centuries. These costumes were faithfully
reproduced in contemporary engravings and paintings. Here
Maria Feodorovna is dressed as a medieval tsarina, with her
brocade robes encrusted with precious stone cabochons.

TWO PHOTOGRAPHS OF GRAND DUCHESS MARIA PAVLOVNA
(opposite). The young Princess Marie of Mecklenburg-Schwerin
married Grand Duke Vladimir Alexandrovich, brother of
Alexander III, to become Grand Duchess Maria Pavlovna. Blessed
with intelligence, character and elegance, she was the unchallenged
queen of St Petersburg society for decades. Every distinguished
figure in the empire and every foreign visitor of any note was
drawn to her salon. Her sister-in-law, Empress Maria Feodorovna,
maintained a state of armed truce with her. Her niece, Empress
Alexandra Feodorovna, wife of Nicholas II, was not so fortunate,
and was the frequent victim of her scathing remarks. In the right-
hand photograph she is shown wearing a circular diamond tiara
with a band of pearl and diamond pendants which may today be
seen incorporated in a tiara belonging to Queen Elizabeth II.
Left: Collection of Prince Dmitri of Yugoslavia.
Right: Private collection, Paris.

MARIA FEODOROVNA'S BOUDOIR in the Gatchina Palace.
Seeking refuge from the threat of attacks by nihilist militants,
Alexander III and his family withdrew from St Petersburg and
went to live in the country, at the Gatchina Palace. Finding the
state apartments too grand and lofty for their tastes, they installed
themselves in a mezzanine with lower ceilings. Edward Hau's
meticulously detailed watercolour of Maria Feodorovna's boudoir
in 1877 depicts a triumph of the late nineteenth-century rococo
style, with portraits of Nicholas I and his wife Alexandra
Feodorovna hanging on the walls.

NICHOLAS II wearing his favourite hussar uniform (opposite), in a portrait
by Alexander Makovsky in 1908. Handsome features, elegantly clipped
beard, a gentle, pensive expression: It is hard to imagine that this sensitive,
shy man, in love with his wife, of simple tastes – all in all, in fact, rather
dull and ordinary – was destined to become the central figure of one of the
greatest tragedies in history.

Nicholas II *1894–1918*

If Alexander III was a giant of a man, his eldest son was quite the opposite: physically
puny and painfully lacking in self-confidence, he was generally held to be weak in
character and devoid of personality. Intriguing, banal, touching and ultimately disastrous, Nicholas II embarked on his reign hampered by the avowed conviction that he was
unfit for sovereignty. The only area in which he had shown any firmness of resolve or
strength of character was in his choice of a wife. The start of his relationship with Princess
Alix of Hesse-Darmstadt was the stuff of a romantic novel. Dispatched to Europe – chiefly
Germany – on a quest for an eligible princess, the Tsarevich had fallen in love with the
young Alix. For complex reasons her family were against the marriage, however, and Alix
herself adamantly and tearfully refused to convert to the Orthodox religion, an absolute
prerequisite for any bride of a future tsar. But finally she was won over, and they were
married – with catastrophic results for both of them.

In her native Hesse, the beautiful and ill-fated Princess Alix was said to 'have the evil
eye'. Certainly her union with Nicholas did not enjoy an auspicious start, for they were
betrothed on the day after Alexander III's death, and the wedding took place while the
court was still in mourning. But everyone was keen to put this ominous beginning behind
them, and to rejoice in the fact that the empire now had at its head a young and handsome
couple who appeared full of goodwill and humanity. The coronation in Moscow was an
affair of solemn magnificence and ancient tradition, transporting guests from the sophis-
tication of the late nineteenth-century to the fabulous splendour of the Russian medieval
court. Yet even this happy occasion was marred by tragedy. The day after the coronation,
it was customary for the new Tsar to distribute gifts to the people, who came in their thousands. On this occasion there was a stampede, which left – according to estimates –
over one thousand five-hundred dead and thousands more injured.

The early years of the young couple's reign and marriage passed relatively unevent-
fully, as they did their best to combine the duties required of them as rulers of the world's
largest empire with their own desire to lead a quiet and contented family life. Court life
continued in a whirl of balls, at which the Tsarina demonstrated a natural sense of style.
She took an active interest in the design of the majority of her gowns, which were of great

MINIATURE OF TSAR NICHOLAS II
(above) on the lid of a snuffbox,
signed A. Blanov, presented by the
Tsar to the French minister Théophile
Delcassé. Sumptuous trinkets such as
this, known as 'diplomatic gifts', were
intended to sweeten relationships
with foreign politicians and diplomats
– for who, after all, could resist a gift
of diamonds?

THE IMPERIAL ORB, symbol of the tsar's earthly power. Probably made by court jeweler Jérémie Pauzié for the coronation of Catherine the Great in 1762, it was used at all subsequent coronations. The orb is of gold decorated with bands of Brazilian diamonds, all of fine quality. The single very large pear-shaped diamond, weighing 46.92 carats, came from the famous Golconda mines in India. The orb is surmounted by an enormous 200-carat sapphire from Ceylon, supported by a diamond cross.
Diamond Fund. Moscow Kremlin.

elegance and suited her to perfection. To the unparalleled collection of jewels that she had inherited she added more, commissioning the Swedish jeweller Bolin especially to set gemstones from the crown jewels in diadems and suites. Adorned with the world's largest and most magnificent tiaras, she would pose for photographers and painters like a saint in an icon, her gaze fixed on the middle distance, majestic and aloof.

The imperial family at this time was studded with a constellation of beauties, including the Tsar's sister Grand Duchess Xenia; Zénaïde de Beauharnais, wife of a distant cousin of Napoleon who appears in photographs sheathed in cabochons; and – most glorious of all – Grand Duchess Sergei, sister to the Tsarina and wife of one of the Tsar's uncles. Known as Ella within the imperial family, the Grand Duchess was a party-loving extrovert who thought nothing of changing her gown and jewels three times within the space of an evening, in a crescendo of dazzling magnificence.

Perhaps the most fabulous of all these glittering court festivities was the masked ball given in 1903. The theme was Russia in the seventeenth century, which offered the ideal pretext for encrusting the dramatic costumes – brocade gowns stiff with gold thread and traditional Russian tunics – with specially created jewels of spectacular proportions.

But sombre times were looming, and soon all this finery would be returned to its caskets and cases for storage. The war with Japan proved disastrous for Russia, and the stage was set for the revolution of 1905, followed by war in Europe and the cataclysm of the 1917 Revolution. Amid all this turmoil, few of his countrymen would have suspected that in order to fund these calamities Nicholas had discreetly sold off a good proportion of the unmounted stones in the crown collection; the astonishing collection of cut diamonds that belonged to the last Nizam of Hyderabad and that were constantly on view in New Delhi, for instance, almost certainly came from this sale.

Grand society hostesses such as the Dowager Empress Maria Feodorovna and the indefatigable Grand Duchess Vladimir did their valiant best to keep up appearances with a constant round of receptions at their respective palaces, but the mood of the times was against them. The Empress Alexandra, moreover, had shut herself away with her family in the Alexander Palace, suffering from nervous hysteria and ill with worry over her son Alexis, whose disabling haemophilia was still a closely guarded secret from the rest of the world. Court balls and receptions were things of the past. The amusements of fashionable society carried on in private circles, but without firm leadership the court became mired in malicious gossip against the Tsar and Tsarina. The imperial couple, meanwhile, spent quiet evenings bent over a handsome notebook, in which they painted watercolours of the cufflinks and cravat pins given to them by relatives. It was trinkets such as these, mostly made by Fabergé, that commanded their admiration, while beside them the largest, finest and most celebrated jewels in the world slumbered on unnoticed.

THE MARRIAGE OF NICHOLAS II AND EMPRESS ALEXANDRA FEODOROVNA in
1894 (above). Official court mourning for the death of Alexander III, six months before,
had to be lifted for twenty-four hours to allow the celebration of these nuptials. The
ceremony took place in the chapel on the top floor of the Winter Palace. Beside the bridal
couple and the Orthodox priests, all clad in gold brocade, Ilya Repin's painting shows the
Dowager Empress Maria Feodorovna, dressed in white, and her own father, Christian IX
of Denmark. Over the heads of the bride and groom, pageboys hold the nuptial crowns
used in Orthodox weddings. Nicholas and Alexandra were not allowed a honeymoon, and
as their apartments in the Winter Palace were not ready they were obliged to make do
with three cramped rooms on the ground floor of the Anitchkov Palace, residence of the
Dowager Empress – who lost no time in embarking on her campaign of persecution of
her daughter-in-law.
State Russian Museum, St Petersburg.

THE IMPERIAL SCEPTRE (opposite). The shaft is of gold, and beneath the double-headed
eagle in gold, enamel and diamonds glitters the famous Orlov diamond. This enormous
stone is reputed to have been used as one of the eyes of a statue of the god Brahma in
Mysore, from where it was stolen by a French deserter who pretended to be a convert to
the Hindu faith. He escaped with it, and is later supposed to have sold it on the
Amsterdam diamond market. The disgraced Prince Grigory Orlov, casting around for a
way back into the favours of his former mistress, Catherine the Great, bought the great
jewel and presented it to her. The Empress accepted his gift and had it mounted on the
imperial sceptre, but never allowed Orlov back into either her good graces or her bed.
Diamond Fund, Moscow Kremlin.

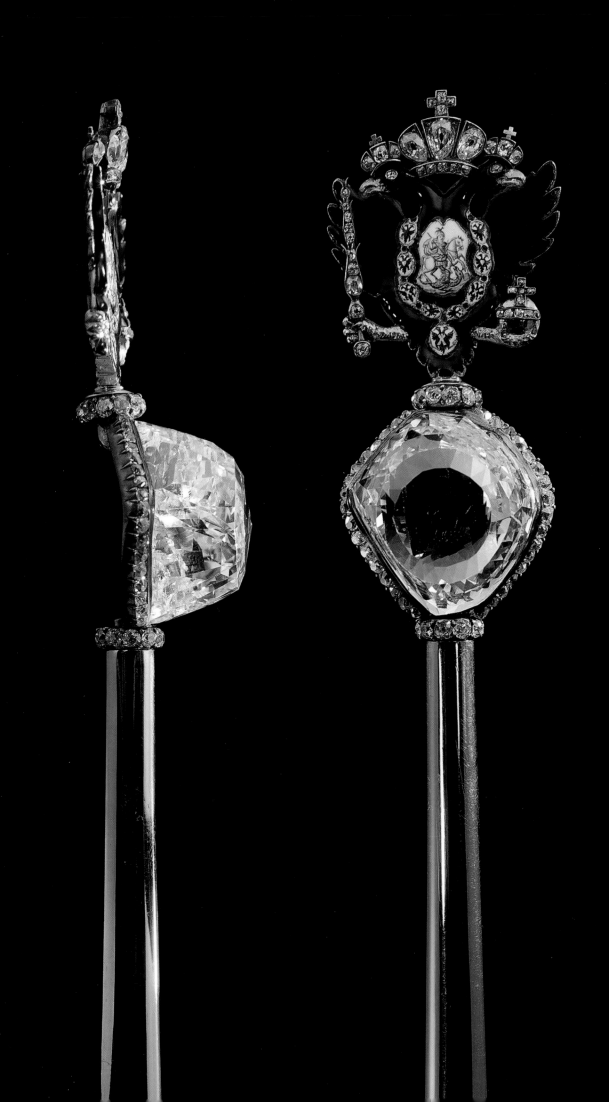

THE CORONATION OF NICHOLAS II AND ALEXANDRA FEODOROVNA, 14 May 1896. This painting by Henri Gervex depicts the moment at which the Tsar places the crown on his own head in the Cathedral of the Assumption within the Moscow Kremlin. On this occasion the Khodynka Meadows on the outskirts of Moscow were chosen as the site for the coronation festivities, and for reasons that remain unclear, a stampede broke out among the crowds of people who had gathered there, leaving over one thousand five-hundred dead. The massacre was seen as a bad omen, and it began to be whispered that the new Empress was the bringer of ill luck – a rumour that can only have appeared to have found confirmation in the sad events of the rest of her life and her tragic death.
Musée d'Orsay, Paris.

Shattering events in the world at large were mirrored by scandals within the imperial family, splintering it into factions and imposing yet further restrictions on fashionable society. That the grand dukes should keep mistresses was to be expected and attracted little unfavorable comment. By far the most successful of these adventuresses, Mathilde Kchessinskaya, boasted among her conquests not only the Tsarevich before he became Nicholas II but also no fewer than three of his cousins, one of whom she eventually married. No one was too concerned that the Grand Dukes Alexis and Boris lived openly with such 'creatures', but when it came to matters of divorce the Tsarina was less tolerant. Her sister-in-law's divorce of her brother, the Grand Duke of Hesse, in order to marry the Tsar's first cousin, Grand Duke Cyril, was a cause of major upset, hurt feelings and furious rows within the family. Then came a flurry of morganatic marriages. First was Grand Duke Mikhail Mikhailovich, who eloped with Countess Sophie von Merenberg; but as he was the younger son of a younger son and she was after all the daughter of a Prince of Nassau and a descendant of the poet Pushkin, they were merely sent into exile and the Countess was given the title Countess of Torby.

Then came Grand Duke Paul, who insisted on marrying a commoner by the name of Olga Karnovich. However, worst of all by far was the case of the Tsar's brother, Grand Duke Mikhail. As the Tsar's only son, Alexis, suffered from haemophilia, his brother was a person of considerable consequence who might one day inherit the throne. Mikhail's infatuation with a divorcee, Natalia Sheremeteviski, caused a deep and lasting rift within the family, though once again the Tsar eventually offered the Grand Duke a reluctant pardon and awarded his wife the title of Countess Brassov.

With the imperial family stumbling from one crisis to another, the Tsarina withdrew with her family into total seclusion: now nobody knew what was going on within the walls of the Alexander Palace, and rumours about the sinister influence of a satanic 'holy man' by the name of Rasputin were rife.

This was the background against which Russia found itself ineluctably drawn into a war that neither Rasputin – who foresaw the worst – nor Nicholas – who loathed conflict – wanted to fight. This was not a time for balls or jewels. A few victories gave way to a string of crushing defeats. Rasputin became the victim of one of the most melodramatic murder plots in history, and the Revolution put a bloody end to the Romanov dynasty. The beautiful Grand Duchess Sergei, who after her husband's death had founded an order of nuns of which she was abbess, was thrown down a mine shaft by revolutionaries. With her were several other members of the imperial family, including the eighteen-year-old son of Grand Duke Paul and Princess Paley, Vladimir Paley, a handsome young poet full of talent and promise. Other grand dukes were shot. And in July 1918, at Ekaterinburg in the Urals, Nicholas, Alexandra and their five children were massacred.

EMPRESS ALEXANDRA FEODOROVNA early in her marriage (opposite). She had just married the love of her life, and in so doing claimed the most prestigious throne in Europe – yet her expression is one of profound melancholy, as though somewhere deep down she foresaw the tragic destiny that lay in store for herself and her beloved husband and children.

DIAMOND TIARA mounted in white gold (above), from the collection of the Grand Dukes of Luxemburg. If today's royal families can boast a Russian imperial ancestor, this may be detected in the splendour of their jewels. This tiara was part of the dowry of Grand Duchess Elizabeth Mikhailovna for her marriage to Prince Adolphe of Nassau, future grand Duke of Luxemburg. The marriage was childless, and the Grand Duke remarried Adelaide of Anhalt, from whom the present royal family are descended. The Russian imperial tiara was worn by Grand Duchess Charlotte of Luxemburg at her marriage to Prince Felix of Bourbon-Parma.

page 126

EMPRESS ALEXANDRA FEODOROVNA, wife of Nicholas II, in 1908. As this portrait by Nikolai Bodarewski shows, Alexandra was not only a great beauty but also extremely elegant. She designed her own gowns, and took a close interest in the execution of the jewels that she commissioned, such as this sapphire and diamond tiara by the Swedish jeweler Bolin. But although adored by her husband and children, she was of a nervous, shy and rather morbid disposition. In public she was awkward and lacked grace, and it was clear that she detested the social whirl of court life and preferred to devote herself exclusively to her family. Although at heart she was good and well-intentioned, she succeeded only in making herself thoroughly and universally unpopular. Her ill-advised decisions and want of judgement undoubtedly contributed to the terrible fate that awaited her and her family.

page 127

THE RED SPINEL weighing 491 carats that surmounts the great imperial crown. This crown belonged to Peter the Great.
Diamond Fund. Moscow Kremlin.

page 128

GRAND DUCHESS ELENA VLADIMIROVNA on the day of her marriage to Prince Nicholas of Greece. The Grand Duchess wears the marriage robes and jewels worn by all the tsarinas and grand duchesses for their weddings: the fastening-pin used to fasten the imperial mantle (see pages 88–9), the diamond rivière, the earrings (page 129), the diamond tiara with the pink diamond of Paul I, and finally the diamond nuptial crown. The crimson velvet and ermine mantle was so heavy that more than one bride, having knelt during the ceremony, found herself pinned to the ground and unable to stagger up again.
Collection of Prince Dmitri of Yugoslavia.

page 129

PAIR OF EARRINGS IN THE FORM OF CHERRIES, in diamonds mounted in gold and silver. Brazilian diamonds such as these are of the first water. Commissioned by Catherine the Great, these earrings were worn by all the tsarinas and grand duchesses on their wedding day.
Diamond Fund, Moscow Kremlin.

TWO IMPERIAL EGGS BY FABERGÉ (opposite & page 133). At the command of Alexander III and later Nicholas II, Fabergé created fabulous Easter eggs which, following the Orthodox tradition, the tsars gave to their wives – and, in Nicholas II's case, to his mother. These legendary eggs of gold, enamel and precious stones were the most priceless objects in the world. Giving free rein to his imagination, Fabergé endowed each one with motifs drawn from the lives of the imperial family. The example (opposite), created for Easter 1908, is decorated on the outside with miniatures of the five children of Nicholas and Alexandra, while it opens up to reveal a 'surprise' in the form of a miniature model in precious metal of the Alexander Palace at Tsarskoë Selo, residence of the Tsar and his family. The egg created in 1913 for the tercentenary of the Romanov dynasty (page 133), is decorated on the outside with miniatures of the Romanov tsars, and contains a globe showing the extent of the Russian empire.
Diamond Fund, Moscow Kremlin.

page 132

VICTORIA MELITA, daughter of Alfred Duke of Edinburgh and Grand Duchess Maria Alexandrovna. Victoria Melita's first husband was Prince Ernst Ludwig of Hesse, brother of the Tsarina. This marriage was then dissolved and she married her first love and first cousin, Grand Duke Kyril Vladimirovich, so scandalizing the courts of Europe and incurring the wrath of Nicholas and Alexandra. Later, when she had been forgiven and accepted back into the imperial family, she was permitted to wear the traditional robes of the grand duchesses with the magnificent imperial jewels.

DOUBLE-HEADED EAGLE IN DIAMONDS (above). For the tercentenary celebrations of the Romanov dynasty in 1913, the imperial court commissioned a wealth of costly souvenirs and keepsakes, such as this double-headed eagle in diamonds, surmounted by the ancient crown of the medieval tsars known as the 'Crown of Monomakh', which fell out of use in the sixteenth century. This jewel was a gift from Empress Alexandra Feodorovna to her lady-in-waiting Baroness Buxhoeveden. During the Revolution the Baroness fled Russia on the roof of a railway carriage, carrying this jewel hidden on her person. She later gave it to Victoria, Princess Louis of Battenberg and sister of the murdered Tsarina. The brooch remains in her family to this day.

GRAND DUCHESS ELIZABETH FEODOROVNA with her lady-in-waiting (opposite). Born Princess Elizabeth of Hesse-Darmstadt, Elizabeth Feodorovna was the sister of Empress Alexandra Feodorovna and married Grand Duke Sergei Alexandrovich, younger brother of Alexander III. When Sergei Alexandrovich, then Governor of Moscow, was killed by an anarchist bomb, Grand Duchess Elizabeth withdrew from society and founded a religious order. Having been a glittering social butterfly and darling of the imperial court, she now lived a life of irreproachable piety and discretion. This did not deter the revolutionaries of 1917 from arresting her and taking her away, before throwing her and others down a mineshaft while still alive, and tossing in grenades to finish them off. Her remains were later transported to Jerusalem, and she was canonized by the Orthodox church.
Collection of Mrs Helmis Markezinis.

EMPRESS ALEXANDRA FEODOROVNA with her son, the Tsarevich Alexis
(opposite). In an artless and touching gesture, the small boy has wound his
mother's pearls round his hand. She, meanwhile, can barely conceal her
overwhelming sadness. Her only son, loving, handsome, intelligent and gifted,
suffered from haemophilia, a congenital and painful disorder that prevents
the blood from clotting, and which therefore put him at grave risk from even
the tiniest scratch. From the time of his birth, his parents lived in a state of
constant and all-consuming anxiety.

MINIATURE OF NICHOLAS II BY FABERGÉ (above). Crowned and encircled by
diamonds, the portrait appears to hang from a gold and enamel column, topped
by a double-headed eagle, symbol of the Russian monarchy. The photograph of
Tsarevich Alexis Nikolaievich in a sailor suit, in an opulent frame, is in the style
of Fabergé, but is in fact made by Fabergé's rival Hahn in 1895.
Reproduced by kind permission of A la Vieille Russie, New York.

DAUGHTER-IN-LAW AND MOTHER-IN-LAW. Empress Alexandra Feodorovna (above) is shown in full ceremonial court dress, with the diamond necklace of the Order of St Andrew on the bodice of her gown. She wears her favourite diamond and pearl tiara by Bolin, and even the buttons of her sumptuous gown are of diamonds and pearls. Her mother-in-law, Empress Maria Feodorovna (opposite), who made no secret of the fact that she cordially detested her daughter-in-law, is photographed in the robes she wore for the coronation of her son Nicholas II. Her fabulous diamond necklace – with peerless stones of a total of 475 carats making it uniquely precious – was sold at the time of the Revolution and lost from sight. On her head she wears a small diamond crown made for this occasion in 1896, which has also vanished completely and mysteriously without trace.

NICHOLAS II'S CORONATION BALL was the occasion for a breathtaking parade of the most superlative jewels in the Russian imperial treasury. This photograph, taken amid the lush palms of the Kremlin winter garden, shows the Dowager Empress, Alexandra Yossifovna, widow of Konstantin Nikolaievich, and on her left the guest of honour, the Duchess of Connaught. The Duchess's granddaughter, Elsa of Württemberg, sits on the floor at her feet. Standing, from left to right are: Elsa's sister Olga of Württemberg; their mother Vera of Russia, Princess Wilhelm of Württemberg; Grand Duchesses Anastasia Mikhailovna; Maria Pavlovna; Elena Vladimirovna and Vera Makrivievna, and on the extreme right Victoria, Crown Princess of Sweden. Behind each of them stands a pageboy whose job it was to hold up their long trains.

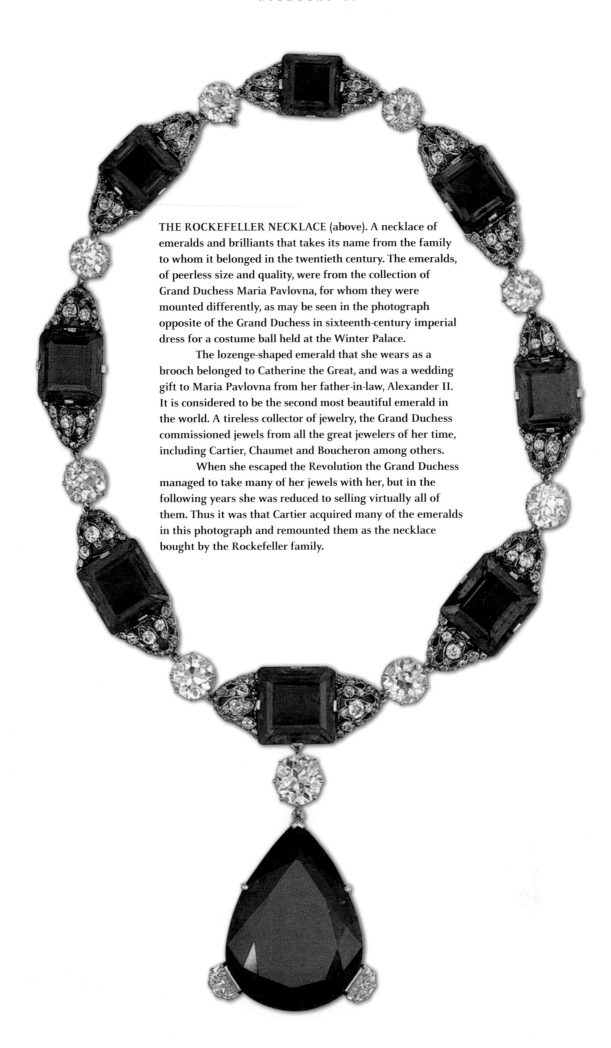

THE ROCKEFELLER NECKLACE (above). A necklace of emeralds and brilliants that takes its name from the family to whom it belonged in the twentieth century. The emeralds, of peerless size and quality, were from the collection of Grand Duchess Maria Pavlovna, for whom they were mounted differently, as may be seen in the photograph opposite of the Grand Duchess in sixteenth-century imperial dress for a costume ball held at the Winter Palace.

The lozenge-shaped emerald that she wears as a brooch belonged to Catherine the Great, and was a wedding gift to Maria Pavlovna from her father-in-law, Alexander II. It is considered to be the second most beautiful emerald in the world. A tireless collector of jewelry, the Grand Duchess commissioned jewels from all the great jewelers of her time, including Cartier, Chaumet and Boucheron among others.

When she escaped the Revolution the Grand Duchess managed to take many of her jewels with her, but in the following years she was reduced to selling virtually all of them. Thus it was that Cartier acquired many of the emeralds in this photograph and remounted them as the necklace bought by the Rockefeller family.

FUR-TRIMMED AND BEJEWELLED HAT worn by Nicholas II for the costume ball of 1903 (above). Even when the imperial court dressed up, the jewels were real. The Tsar's cap is of gold brocade trimmed with sable and strewn with pearls, emeralds and rubies.
Renaissance design. Moscow Kremlin.

NICHOLAS AND ALEXANDRA (opposite), despite their horror of society occasions, decided to give a costume ball at the Winter Palace in 1903, to which guests would come in sixteenth-century Russian dress. They themselves appeared in the robes of a medieval tsar and tsarina, in sumptuous brocades encrusted with huge precious stones.

pages 146–7
PHOTOGRAPHS OF THE FAMOUS BALL of 1903 were collected together in a magnificent album. In their splendid costumes, and decked out with precious jewels, the guests all look as if they have stepped out of a gallery of sixteenth-century portraits. The majority of the figures photographed in all their splendour were to meet tragic ends, either murdered by the revolutionaries or condemned to perpetual exile. The photograph of the Grand Duchess Xenia Alexandrovna, sister of Nicholas II, and her husband, Grand Duke Alexander Mikhailovich (page 146), is framed by flowers of diamonds mounted in silver which were used as trimmings on Catherine the Great's ceremonial gowns.

Grand Duke Mikhail Alexandrovich, younger brother of Nicholas II (pictured on page 147 in a coat embroidered with small pearls, and a jerkin, hat and dagger handle encrusted with enormous cut stones) was to make a morganatic marriage with – to make matters even worse – a divorcee. When Nicholas II abdicated at the start of the Revolution, he named Mikhail as his successor. Mikhail reigned for a day before abdicating in turn, and was then killed by the Bolsheviks. His wife and son later died in poverty in Paris.

VIEW OF THE PARK AT PETERHOF (opposite). Built by Peter the Great, the palace of Peterhof was to remain the favourite summer residence of all the tsars who followed him, with the whole court decamping there during the hottest months of the year. Nicholas II and his family stayed there until the eve of the revolution, when they were arrested, taken away and massacred. The palace stood empty and abandoned, until it was virtually destroyed by the Germans during the Second World War. Magnificently reconstructed and meticulously restored down to its finest details by the Soviet authorities, it is now one of the most visited museums in Russia. This watercolour by Ivan Aivasovsky shows the park in 1837, with its cascades and fountains feeding into a canal that flowed into the Baltic.

page 150
THE OPENING OF THE DUMA on 27 April 1906. The Revolution of 1917 had been foreshadowed by a dress rehearsal in the form of the 1905 Revolution, which started with the notorious Bloody Sunday in October of that year, when police and Cossacks opened fire on a workers' procession, and spread to every corner of the empire. It led to the establishment of the first Russian parliament, the Duma, which was solemnly opened by Nicholas II in the great St George's Hall of the Winter Palace. Here he is shown entering the hall with his mother, Maria Feodorovna, on his right and his wife, Alexandra Feodorovna, on his left. For the occasion, the two empresses have donned full court dress, complete with tiaras, lace veils and brocade trains, in stark contrast to the 'bourgeois' simplicity of the newly elected members.

Haunted by the oath he had sworn on his accession to defend the divine right of the monarchy, Nicholas was convinced that he had betrayed his autocracy by accepting this move towards democracy, which was viewed as a humiliation by the empresses, other members of the imperial family and the court.

page 151
GRAND DUCHESSES OLGA AND TATIANA NIKOLAIEVNA with their two younger sisters and their haemophiliac brother, the two eldest daughters of Nicholas and Alexandra formed a strongly united family. The jewels worn by the Grand Duchesses are extremely simple in comparison with the confections sported by their predecessors. Olga was supposed to have been betrothed to the Crown prince of Romania, but refused on any account to leave her native Russia to live abroad. Thus it was that she shared the fate of the rest of her family, brutally murdered at Ekaterinburg in July 1918.

THE BOLSHEVIK GOVERNMENT set up a commission to make an inventory of the imperial jewels and estimate their value with a view to their possible sale. This photograph (left), published in the periodical *L'Illustration* in 1922, shows the members of the commission around a table on which the jewels are spread out. Clearly identifiable is the tiara of which a replica is reproduced on page 62.

After 1917

One night at the height of the Revolution, the grandson of Carl Fabergé was roughly shaken from sleep by the secret police. As they took him away he was convinced that his last hour had come: after all, his name perhaps more than any other symbolized both capitalism and empire in Russia.

In fact he was brought before Trotsky, who quite courteously requested him to make a complete valuation of all the imperial jewels. The Revolution, he explained, needed money, and the plan was to empty the imperial coffers and sell the contents. The young Fabergé spent weeks working under the watchful eye of Bolshevik guards. When he presented Trotsky with his report, however, he discovered that there had been a change of plan. The smallest and least significant pieces, unmounted stones, and jewels of no historical value would be sold, but everything of historical value would be kept. The Revolution killed off the tsars, but it would not deny the existence of Russia's imperial past.

A 'Diamond Chamber' was created within the Kremlin to house a display of the crowns, sceptres, orbs and diadems that had served successive sovereigns. So strong was this attachment to the past, indeed, that even in the Soviet era young designers used genuine gemstones to create replicas of the jewels that were assumed to have been sold.

In 1922, a spectacular sale of Russian imperial jewels took place at Christie's in London. Among this random haul of diadems, tiaras, necklaces, earrings, brooches and

AN EXTREMELY RARE PHOTOGRAPH (above) which the Soviet government attempted unsuccessfully to suppress. During a break from the commission's work, a worker is captured parodying the Tsar by crowning himself with the imperial crown and grasping the orb in one hand and the sceptre in the other. Lampoons of this sort did not amuse the Bolsheviks, however, even when the joke was at the expense of their former masters.

PORTRAIT OF QUEEN MARIE OF ROMANIA by Laszlo. Daughter of Alfred, Duke of Edinburgh and Grand Duchess Maria Alexandrovna, Queen Marie had a passion for jewels. In the aftermath of the Russian Revolution, she bought numerous jewels from members of the imperial family, starting with her sister (page 132), who had married a Grand Duke. Photographs and paintings of Marie therefore show her sporting many pieces previously worn by empresses and grand duchesses. Fancying herself rather as a medieval sovereign, she liked to have her portrait taken in suitably evocative outfits.

bracelets were some that were to remain intact, such as the pearl and diamond tiara bought by Gladys, Duchess of Marlborough, which was later to find its way into the collections of Imelda Marcos.

But the great majority of these jewels were destined to be broken up, the customary fate at the time of jewels that had been sold, so that they would be beyond recognition. Although the imperial Russian jewels were not merely displays of fabulous gemstones but also masterpieces of the goldsmith's art, this was of little concern to those who bought them. All that now remains of most of these fabulous jewels are the superb black-and-white photographs reproduced in the famous Fersman catalogue. Many of these unmounted stones were so celebrated for their beauty, their size, their brilliance or their history, however, that even through several different incarnations in which they may have been recut and remounted, we can still trace their chequered careers.

The imperial jewels survived the Revolution, as did some members – mostly women – of the Romanov dynasty. Those who managed to survive the terrible ordeals to which they were subjected fled abroad, taking with them as many of their jewels as they could carry. All of these were then sold.

The Dowager Empress Maria Feodorovna managed to take with her a bag full of what she termed 'everyday' jewels, which to our eyes would be magnificent enough for the grandest of occasions. They were to be sold by her daughters Xenia and Olga.

Another considerable cache was smuggled out by Grand Duchess Maria Pavlovna and her daughter-in-law Grand Duchess Victoria Feodorovna, who to the fury of the Tsarina had divorced the Grand Duke of Hesse in order to marry a cousin of the Tsar. Many of these jewels remained intact, and the present Queen of England may now be seen wearing tiaras and brooches that once belonged to a grand duchess or tsarina.

Over time, however, all these sources ran dry, and the surviving Romanovs were left with no jewels either to sell or to wear. Families who can boast a Romanov forebear, by contrast, can equally invariably boast a dazzling array of jewels. The royal families of Sweden, Holland and Wurtemberg, and the German princely families of Schaumberg-Lippe and Mecklenburg, together with various branches of the house of Saxe, have all been fortunate enough to have inherited a considerable quantity of Russian imperial jewels, and

THE NUPTIAL CROWN OF THE RUSSIAN IMPERIAL FAMILY, made by the jewellers Nicholls Planke in the 1840s using diamond trimmings taken from the gowns of Catherine the Great. Worn for their weddings by all the empresses and grand duchesses (see page 28), it was sold through Christie's by the Bolsheviks in 1927, and is one of only a very few jewels sold during the Revolution to have survived intact. It was bought by Mrs Marjorie Merriweather Post, an American millionairess who was a passionate and pioneering collector of imperial Russian artefacts, whose husband was posted to Russia in the Soviet era. *Hillwood Museum Collection.*

to have held on to them to the present day. Sometimes they are forced to part with a piece, and it is never without emotion that surviving members of the family contemplate a Romanov jewel coming up for sale at public auction.

Many of the imperial jewels are now lost, not so much as a result of the Soviet era as through sales, dispersal, disappearance, theft and war. But those that have survived, and that we may still admire today – worn by monarchs or the wives of millionaires – are still so fabulous that they remain the stuff of dreams. These are the dazzling remains of the greatest treasure trove the world has ever known, glittering mementoes of the princesses, grand duchesses and tsarinas who wore them on their heads, their throats and their wrists, through the dramas of love and glory, virtue and tragedy that defined the remarkable lives of the Romanovs.

THE ENIGMA OF THE LOST JEWELS

The fate of many of the Russian imperial jewels, both during and after the Revolution, remains tantalizingly shrouded in mystery. Take for instance the great sales organised by the Soviet authorities in the 1920s. The famous Fersman catalogue, commissioned by the Soviet government and a bible to amateurs, includes a number of outstanding jewels that are not to be found either among those kept in Russia on Trotsky's orders or in the catalogues to the numerous sales held abroad. Who kept them? What happened to them? Nobody knows.

After being imprisoned in their own palace at Tsarskoë Selo, the imperial family – Nicholas II, Alexandra and their five children – was sent to Tobolsk in Siberia. They did not go empty-handed: an entire carriage of the special train that took them to Siberia was hardly enough to contain all their luggage. At Tobolsk they continued to be treated relatively well. Then some of them were moved again, this time to Ekaterinburg in the Urals. By some means still unknown to us, those who had left managed to get a message back to those still at Tobolsk. It contained a warning that there had been a marked deterioration in the conditions in which they were being held, and that among other measures those at Tobolsk must at all costs conceal most of the jewels that they had managed to bring with them. According to some accounts, Alexandra summoned a number of local nuns or monks and entrusted them with two or three enormous jars filled with jewels. Then the Tsarina and her remaining children were dispatched to Ekaterinburg in their turn.

TIARA OF DIAMONDS mounted in gold and silver, in the form of ears of corn and foliage. Made for Maria Feodorovna, wife of Paul I, it was worn by all subsequent tsarinas. This photograph shows a replica of the original, which was sold during the Revolution and dismantled. So attached were the Soviet authorities to relics of the empire that they had overthrown, however, that they commissioned an exact copy of it. *Diamond Fund, Moscow Kremlin.*

Some time later, when the convent in which one of the jars was hidden was disbanded by the revolutionaries, the abbess entrusted the jewels to a peasant or gardener. This unfortunate man was denounced and, probably under torture, revealed the hiding place. The jar was duly found, and its contents photographed and inventoried by the Soviet authorities. Then these too vanished. The fate of the other two jars of jewels, which specialists believe were never found, also remains unknown. Perhaps they still lie in some unlikely hiding spot in Tobolsk ....

Finally, in a grotesque detail, we know that during the massacre of the imperial family at Ekaterinburg the bullets fired by the assassins had difficulty in piercing the bodies of the Grand Duchesses. This was simply because the linings of their corsets contained jewels and gemstones which they had stitched into them, in the poignant hope that they might one day help them out in hard times. After the massacre these jewels were discovered: although generally of little significance, they included one or two important pieces, such as an emerald cross and some unmounted diamonds.

When the White Russian forces arrived at Ekaterinburg and opened an enquiry into the massacre of the imperial family, they were taken to a mine shaft into which had been thrown not the victims' bodies, but their belongings. The jewels were recovered and photographed for publication in the famous Sokolov report on the death of the Tsar and his family. Then they were packed up with other personal possessions of the imperial family discovered in Ipatiev House at Ekaterinburg – icons, books, poems and photographs – and sent to Vladivostok, then the only route out of Russia still open. The intention was to ship them on to the late Tsar's relatives and loyal friends in England. But when the packing case was opened at Vladivostok, everything was in place except the jewels. Who had stolen them, how and where? Nobody has ever found out.

Like all the great tragedies of history, the fate of the Russian imperial family is impossible to grasp in all its enormity. So many elements of the Romanovs' extraordinary story still remain shrouded in mystery – and it is not beyond the bounds of possibility that one day some of the fabulous treasure trove of jewels that were such an important part of their legend will come to light once more.

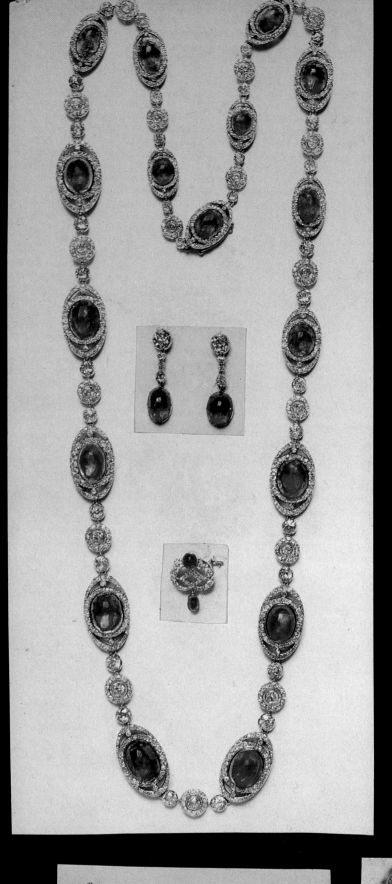

PRINCESS IRINA OF RUSSIA (above). A first cousin of Nicholas II, Irina married Prince Felix Yusupov, later leader of the plot to kill Rasputin. For her wedding, the imperial family showered Irina with sumptuous jewels, which were documented with photographs. When she fled the Revolution, these photographs were all she managed to take with her. Decades later Prince Yusupov, nearing the end of his life, liked to hand-colour these monochrome images in order to remind himself of the colours of the stones: blue sapphires, red rubies and green emeralds (opposite).
Collection of Yusupov and Irina's great-granddaughter, Mrs Xenia Sfiri.

A KOKOSHNIK (opposite), the traditional Russian headdress favoured by ladies of the imperial court, covered with cloth of gold decorated with two rows of round pearls, several very large pear-shaped pearls and some Brazilian diamonds of the finest water. After the Revolution, the imperial jewels were valued, largely at Trotsky's instigation, by Agathon Fabergé. Later, in 1922, they were photographed and described in a sumptuous catalogue produced by Professor A. E. Fersman. Most of them were sold and subsequently broken up. The Fersman catalogue therefore represents the last proof of the existence of these superlative pieces. The images on this and many of the following pages are reproduced from the celebrated Fersman catalogue.

page 164
DIAMOND TIARA adorned with eighteen very large pear-shaped pearls (above) and an emerald and diamond tiara (below) made by Bolin for Empress Alexandra Feodorovna. She is shown wearing it in the portrait on page 124.

Page 165
TINTED PHOTOGRAPH OF OLGA KARNIKOVA, PRINCESS PALEY, in traditional Russian dress. This beautiful divorcee was descended from Hungarian nobles who emigrated to Russia in the seventeenth century. She married Grand Duke Paul of Russia, widower of Alexandra of Greece, and they had three children. The Princess survived the Revolution, but her husband was shot and her son, then only nineteen years old, handsome and a poet of immense promise, was brutally murdered by the Bolsheviks.
Collection of Prince Michael of Russia.

pages 166–7
FRANÇOISE OF FRANCE, PRINCESS CHRISTOPHER OF GREECE. This photograph shows the Princess wearing a tiara and necklace of turquoises encircled by diamonds, exact replicas of pieces in the Russian imperial collection documented in the Fersman catalogue (page 167). These replicas were made for Grand Duchess Olga of Russia, Queen of Greece, who bequeathed them to her son Christopher.

A DIAMOND NECKLACE made up of thirty-six stones of outstanding quality and size, together weighing 475 carats.

GRAND DUCHESS ELENA VLADIMIROVNA, wife of Prince Nicholas of Greece. As Grand Duchess Elena had lived outside Russia since her marriage before the Revolution, she managed to save most of the Russian imperial jewels that she had received as gifts. In this portrait by Laszlo (opposite), the fashionable Hungarian portrait painter of the 1930s, she is shown wearing a diamond tiara encrusted with emeralds. The portrait now belongs to her grandson, Prince Michael of Kent.

pages 170–171
TIARA AND NECKLACE FROM A DIAMOND AND SAPPHIRE PARURE.

THE ROMANIAN PRINCESSES Elizabeth, Queen of Greece, and Marie, Queen of Yugoslavia, at the coronation of their parents, King Ferdinand and Queen Marie of Romania. Behind them are Princess Irene of Greece, their cousin, the Infanta Beatrice, their aunt and their mother's sister. All these princesses descended from the tsars sport Russian imperial jewels, especially Queen Marie of Yugoslavia, resplendent in the foreground in a remarkable emerald and diamond parure. Made by the Swedish jeweller Bolin, these jewels were a gift from Grand Duchess Elizabeth Feodorovna to her niece, Grand Duchess Marie, on the occasion of her marriage to Prince William of Sweden. In straitened circumstances after the Revolution, Grand Duchess Marie was forced to put them up for sale, when they were bought by Alexander I of Yugoslavia as a gift for his wife. Later the parure was sold by Peter II of Yugoslavia to Van Cleef and Arpels.

CORSAGE TRIMMINGS OF CABOCHON EMERALDS SET IN DIAMOND BOWS (opposite).

page 176
DOWAGER EMPRESS MARIA FEODOROVNA. Miraculously, Dowager Empress Maria Feodorovna managed to survive the Revolution. She died an exile in her native Denmark in 1928, still refusing to accept that her son Nicholas II and his family had been assassinated. Her unshakable belief in their survival went with her to the grave. This is probably the last photograph ever to have been taken of her. The Empress who used to deck herself in jewels from top to toe is shown devoid of jewellery, being helped down from her carriage by her faithful Cossack, who remained loyal to the end.

page 177
PRINCESS NATALIA PALEY, child of the morganatic marriage between Grand Duke Paul and Princess Paley. With her glamorous looks, she was able to earn a living after the Revolution as a fashion model. She married the couturier Lucien Lelong. *Reproduced by kind permission of Alexander Vassiliev.*

page 178
MATHILDE KSCHESSINSKAYA, prima ballerina of the St Petersburg Imperial Ballet. Having shared her favours with Nicholas II and two of the grand dukes, she was showered by them with jewels from the imperial treasury. She loved to festoon herself with them, sometimes even to dance. After the Revolution she finally married one of her lovers, Grand Duke Andrei Vladimirovich, and lived by giving dancing lessons and selling her jewels. She died in 1971.

page 179
PRINCESS OLGA OF YUGOSLAVIA, daughter of Grand Duchess Elena Vladimirovna, photographed by Cecil Beaton wearing a necklace, earrings and brooch in diamonds and rubies from the imperial collection. The photograph is now in the possession of her grandson, Prince Dmitri of Yugoslavia.
Reproduced by kind permission of Prince Dmitri of Yugoslavia.

page 180
QUEEN MARY also loved jewels with a passion, and took advantage of the Russian debacle to pick up for a song numerous pieces salvaged by the grand duchesses. Here she wears a pearl and diamond tiara that formerly belonged to Grand Duchess Maria Pavlovna, the elements of which may be seen in her photograph on page 113.

page 181
HELEN OF GREECE, QUEEN OF ROMANIA, wife of Carol I and mother of the present king, Michael I. She wears a diamond tiara *à la grècque* from the Russian imperial jewels, given to her by her mother-in-law Queen Marie of Romania, who in turn had bought it from her own sister, Grand Duchess Victoria Feodorovna.

page 182
PRINCESS NATALIA ROMANOV. While the cousins and nieces of the tsar wore the jewels they had saved from the Revolution in their adopted countries, members of the imperial family lived in a state of destitution. Only one Romanov managed to live on in the Soviet Union, even surviving the Stalinist regime, and that was the granddaughter of Grand Duke Nicholas Konstantinovich. By adopting the name of her father-in-law, Androssov, she somehow managed to elude the KGB. Earning a living as a circus artist, she led a bohemian life in Moscow, as this photograph testifies. She lived long enough to see the fall of the Soviet regime, and to see her rights as a member of the imperial dynasty fully restored.

Mary R 1924

Lambert Weston

PRINCESS NATALIA ROMANOV (above). Caption on page 174.

PRECIOUS STONES FROM THE FORMER IMPERIAL TREASURY (opposite).
During the Revolution, most of the imperial jewels were sold and broken up.
The stones were sometimes recut and invariably reset in order to make it
harder to identify them. The most outstanding examples passed through the
hands of the famous jeweller and dealer in precious stones Harry Winston.
Here he is shown holding in the palm of his hand a 62-carat emerald that
formerly belonged to Grand Duke Boris, and the great 337-carat sapphire
that was once Catherine the Great's.
Courtesy of The House of Harry Winston.

NICHOLAS II in the costume of a seventeenth-century tsar
Diamond Fund. Moscow Kremlin.

Catherine II, Empress of Russia, 1729–1796
m. Peter III, 1728–1762

Paul I, 1754–1776
m. Marie of Württemberg

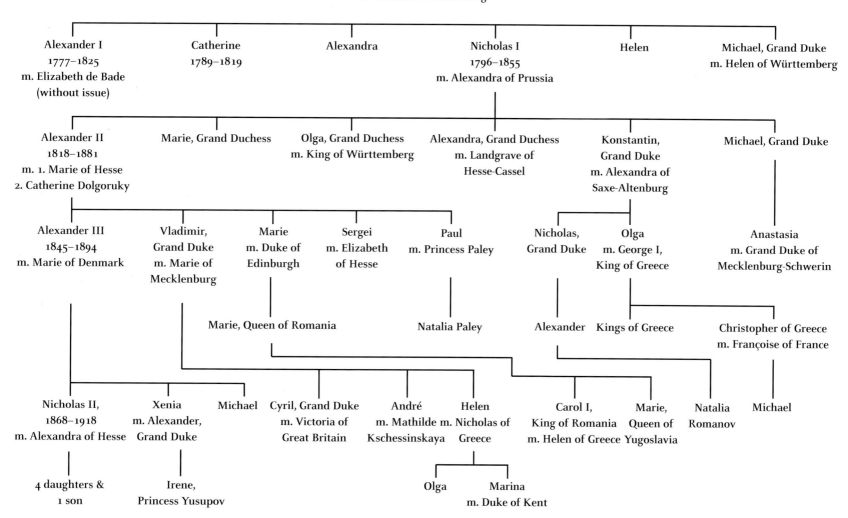

Alexander I
1777–1825
m. Elizabeth de Bade
(without issue)

Catherine
1789–1819

Alexandra

Nicholas I
1796–1855
m. Alexandra of Prussia

Helen

Michael, Grand Duke
m. Helen of Württemberg

Alexander II
1818–1881
m. 1. Marie of Hesse
2. Catherine Dolgoruky

Marie, Grand Duchess

Olga, Grand Duchess
m. King of Württemberg

Alexandra, Grand Duchess
m. Landgrave of
Hesse-Cassel

Konstantin,
Grand Duke
m. Alexandra of
Saxe-Altenburg

Michael, Grand Duke

Alexander III
1845–1894
m. Marie of Denmark

Vladimir,
Grand Duke
m. Marie of
Mecklenburg

Marie
m. Duke of
Edinburgh

Sergei
m. Elizabeth
of Hesse

Paul
m. Princess Paley

Nicholas,
Grand Duke

Olga
m. George I,
King of Greece

Anastasia
m. Grand Duke of
Mecklenburg-Schwerin

Marie, Queen of Romania

Natalia Paley

Alexander   Kings of Greece

Christopher of Greece
m. Françoise of France

Nicholas II,
1868–1918
m. Alexandra of Hesse

Xenia
m. Alexander,
Grand Duke

Michael

Cyril, Grand Duke
m. Victoria of
Great Britain

André
m. Mathilde
Kschessinskaya

Helen
m. Nicholas of
Greece

Carol I,
King of Romania
m. Helen of Greece

Marie,
Queen of
Yugoslavia

Natalia
Romanov

Michael

4 daughters &
1 son

Irene,
Princess Yusupov

Olga

Marina
m. Duke of Kent

Not all the names mentioned in the genealogical tree are illustrated within the book.

Picture Credits

pp. 5, 6, 13, 14, 15, 17, 21, 23, 27, 37, 39 (right), 40, 45 (below), 46, 47, 53, 55, 59, 60, 65, 69, 70, 75, 79, 84, 87, 88–89, 92, 101, 105, 107, 119, 121, 127, 129, 131, 133, 144, 159, 184: Photos by Nikolai Rachmanov.

pp. 8, 18, 33, 34, 44, 68, 71, 74, 81, 117, 136, 138, 139, 143, 145, 146, 147, 153, 155, 176, 178, 182: © Rights reserved.

pp. 12, 20, 36, 38, 41 (left): © State Hermitage Museum, St. Petersburg.

pp. 16, 28, 95, 137: © La vieille Russie, New York.

p. 19: © Swedish National Museum of Fine Arts, Stockholm.

pp. 24, 26, 35, 58, 63, 67, 94, 96–97, 110, 114–115, 120, 123, 126, 150, 151: © Akg-images.

p. 25: © Kugel.

pp. 29, 61, 78, 82–83, 85, 90, 93, 142, 188–189: © Sotheby's.

pp. 30, 32, 39 (left), 41 (right), 48, 62, 102, 108–109: Photos by Olga Fomina.

pp. 31, 49, 64, 91, 103, 111, 113, 116, 125, 132, 134, 135, 140–141, 172–173: Private collections.

p. 45 (above): © S. J. Phillips, London.

pp. 50–51: Collection of the Marquess of Londonderry.

pp. 42–43, 56–57, 72–73, 76–77, 86, 148–149, 160: Francesco Venturi.

pp. 98, 99: © National History Museum, Frederiksborg, Denmark.

p. 106: © Benaki Museum, Athens.

pp. 112, 128, 179: Collection of Prince Dimitri of Yugoslavia.

p. 124: © Sotheby's/akg-images.

p. 135: Collection of Mrs Helmis Markezinis.

p. 152: *L'Illustration*, 1922.

p. 157: © Hillwood Museum & Gardens, Washington.

p. 161: Collection of Mrs Xenia Sfiri.

pp. 163, 164, 166, 167, 168, 170, 171, 175: Catalogue A. E. Fersman.

p. 165: Collection of Prince Michael of Russia.

p. 169: Collection of Prince Michael of Kent.

p. 177: Alexandre Vassiliev.

pp. 180, 181, 186: Collection of Prince Michael of Greece.

p. 183: Bernard Hoffman – Life © 1952 Time, Inc.

Index

page 186
AN ICON DEPICTING NICHOLAS II,
Alexandra Feodorovna and their five children. In a
curious reversal of fortune, the lot of the imperial
family has come full circle: from veneration as autocratic
sovereigns to brutal assassination under the Revolution,
and from oblivion during the Communist era, which
airbrushed them from history, to sainthood conferred
by the Orthodox church. Now their portraits are to be
found on the inexpensive icons that are sold on the
streets of cities where they once held court.

page 190
MARIA ALEXANDROVNA, Empress of Russia and
wife of Alexander II, in her coronation robes, from the
coronation souvenir album.

page 191
ALEXANDER II in his coronation robes, from the
coronation souvenir album.

Acknowledgements

The Duchess of Abercorn,
Mr Georges Antaki,
Lady Mary Bury GP,
Lady Butler CVO,
Mr François Curiel,
The Princess Natalia Vassiltchikov and Christie's,
Mr Jacques Ferrand, Mrs Aimilia Geroulanou and the Benaki Museum,
Landgrave von Hesse,
Lady Pamela Hicks,
Princess Beatrice von Hohenlohe,
Mr Max Karkegi,
Dr Kasinev and Mr Hee Gwone Yoo, the Baltic and Slavic Division of the New York Public Library,
T. R. H. Prince and Princess Michael of Kent,
The Marquess of Londonderry,
Mrs Helmis Markezinis,
Mr Guy May, Commissaire to the Court of Luxembourg,
Mr Andrei Maylunas,
Mrs Suzy Menkes,
The Countess Mountbatten of Burma,
Mr Geoffrey Munn and Wartski,
Mr Xavier Narbaits,
Mrs Magdalena Ribbing,
H. R. H. Prince Michael of Russia,
Mr Pierre Scapula,
Mrs Diane Scarisbrick,
Mr Peter Schaffer, À la Vieille Russie, New York,
Mrs Fabienne de Seze and Harry Winston,
Mrs Xenia Sfiri,
Mr Alexander von Solodkoff,
Mr Stefano Papi, Mrs Alexandra Rhodes and Sotheby's,
Mr Tonnelot and Boucheron,
Mr Alexander Vassiliev,
Mrs Charlotte Wall,
Prince and Princess Alexander of Yugoslavia,
Prince Dimitri of Yugoslavia.

The Hillwood Museum of Mrs Post, The Victoria and Albert Museum,
London and other museums.

Finally, thanks to Victor Loupan, François Sargologo and Séverine Courtaud.